LEARN TO
Meditate

LEARN TO
Meditate

find deep relaxation
relieve stress and anxiety
enhance creativity

DAVID FONTANA

DUNCAN BAIRD PUBLISHERS

LONDON

Learn to Meditate
David Fontana

First published in the United Kingdom and Ireland in 1999 by
Duncan Baird Publishers Ltd
Sixth Floor, Castle House
75–76 Wells Street
London W1T 3QH

Conceived, created and designed by
Duncan Baird Publishers

This revised edition first published in 2009

Managing Editor: Judy Barratt
Editor: Molly Perham with Rebecca Miles
Managing Designer: Gabriella Le Grazie
Designer: Sonya Merali
with Dawn Davies-Cook and Jen Harte
Commissioned artwork: Claire Bushe, Rosamund Fowler
Picture research: Fiona Hill

British Library Cataloguing-in-Publication Data:
A CIP record for this book is available from the British Library

ISBN: 978-1-84483-791-5

3 5 7 9 10 8 6 4 2

Typeset in Mrs Eaves
Colour reproduction by Colourscan, Singapore
Printed in Hong Kong by Imago

Publishers' note
The information in this book is not intended as a substitute for professional
medical advice and treatment. If you are pregnant or are suffering from any medical
conditions or health problems, it is recommended that you consult a medical professional
before following any of the advice or practice suggested in this book. Duncan Baird Publishers,
or any other persons who have been involved in working on this publication, cannot accept
responsibility for any injuries or damage incurred as a result of following the information,
exercises or therapeutic techniques contained in this book.

The abbreviations CE and BCE are used throughout this book:
CE Common Era (the equivalent of AD)
BCE Before the Common Era (the equivalent of BC)

Meditation is the experience of the limitless

nature of the mind when it ceases to be

dominated by its usual mental chatter.

David Fontana

Contents

Part II

Beyond the Gateway

The Great Traditions

Vision and Sound

The Way of Paradox

The Outer Limits

Introduction

This book is intended for those who have no experience of meditation, as well as for experienced meditators who have taken the decision to expand their knowledge of the practice. Its aims are to discuss the theory and practice of meditation, to explain the potential benefits, and to give guidance to help readers to make satisfactory progress on the path toward enlightenment.

If you are a beginner, it is very important to read through Part I (*The Gateless Gate*) before you begin meditation – this section will give you the essential information that you need to make a bold start on your journey.

Over time, a number of meditation techniques have been built up in different cultures around the world. We have tried to explain most of them in this book, giving you a grounding in all the great traditions. However, we do not suggest that you try them all. Different techniques appeal to and suit different people, and it is up to you to decide which ones are best for you – choose those with which you feel most comfortable, least self-conscious and most confident. One particular practice is not necessarily better than another: fundamentally, the basics behind all the major practices are the same – it is only the details, and some of the belief systems underlying them, that differ.

Please note that this book does not make claims for meditation as a treatment for any particular psychological or physical problems. If you are looking for ways in which meditation can help such problems you should refer to a suitably qualified practitioner who will be able to offer you the best remedies. Ultimately, meditation is an intensely personal experience, and people respond to it in different ways.

If you have a psychological or medical condition that you think might be *worsened* by meditation, again you should seek qualified advice before commencing. It is very rare for anyone to experience adverse effects from meditation, but it can happen, and if you have any anxieties before you begin, or once you have started, you should wait, or stop the practice, and seek specialist advice.

The decision to embark upon meditation should not be taken too lightly. Meditation is a serious practice that, for the best results, requires commitment, determination and patience. So why then would we start meditating? Even the most everyday reasons, such as to calm the mind, to give us clarity in daily life, to be more thoughtful of others, are ways of "being" to which most of us aspire. And if it seems like a lot of hard work, remember that these and many other benefits can be achieved, at least in a small way, by the single act of stilling the mind. Mental chatter has become such a habit for most of us that stopping it even for very short periods of time does not come easily — which is why some Zen masters referred to this chatter as the "gate". When first we try to meditate, the gate

appears firmly closed. The mind, although we think it belongs to us, seems to have a stubborn will of its own. But with the help of the techniques we shall be exploring together — and a dose of patience — the gate is progressively seen as the unreal barrier that actually exists, and miraculously we find ourselves through it and embarked upon our meditative journey.

Once you have read this book right through, don't put it aside as if you have no other use for it. Keep it close at hand so that you can refer back to it from time to time to refresh your memory of alternative techniques, and to draw inspiration from its images and ideas.

Meditation is a continual learning curve. We don't need to journey very far to begin to benefit from the experience of meditation, but we need to have commitment if we are to reach advanced levels of mental strength. Nevertheless, for many of us, the simple act of emptying our heads is like refreshing ourselves mentally and physically.

How to Use This Book

In order to best help meditators reach a deep level of contemplation, *Learn to Meditate*, through appropriate methods, the teachings of the great traditions, and suggestions on how to find the right meditation teachers, is divided into two major parts. The first part is primarily for those who are new to meditation; the second part is more advanced.

Part I: The Gateway

Through the gateway of the "gateless gate" lies meditation. The term "gateless gate" is a Japanese *mumonkan* — a Zen saying that at first glance seems nonsensical, but the reality of which is profound: the gate is at once a "thing" (to pass through) and a "no-thing" (the distractions that hinder heightened mental awareness). If meditation lies beyond the gateless gate, then we have to reach the other side before we can attain certain levels of contemplation and insight. Nothing comes between us and the ability to meditate except the thinking, planning and remembering that most of us habitually allow to dominate in our mental lives.

The book's first chapter ("A Path Without End") is a detailed introduction to the ways of meditation, what it is for and where it comes from. If you are a beginner, take time to mull over this background information: if it is well remembered and well understood, it will help you to affirm why you should persevere if at any time your progress seems slow or difficult. Don't be afraid to come back to these introductory pages at any stage.

In chapter two ("Entrances"), we look at the practicalities of learning to meditate. Where should we sit? How long should we spend meditating? What should we wear? Use this chapter as a guide: once you have gained confidence, experiment with your own ideas to create your own perfect meditation scenario. Once chosen, stick to your setting as it will help to put you in the right frame of mind at the beginning of each meditation session.

Chapter three discusses in detail the "Essentials" of meditation, such as focusing the mind to control wayward thoughts and emotions. Try to remain patient with yourself throughout this section (for many of us, learning to meditate means undoing the habits of a lifetime): take it slowly and progressively.

Part II: Beyond the Gateway

Meditation has taken many forms across the world. Through a brief overview of each of the great traditions, we gain some valuable insights into how advanced meditation can be achieved. Use this section as a guide to which of the traditional methods might best suit you – or which elements of each you might like to include in your own practice.

In "Vision and Sound" we hone in upon some of the methods of the various traditions. Again, it is important to persevere even when you find things difficult and, if necessary, go back to the more basic techniques of Part I to re-establish

self-confidence. If you find that one tradition simply doesn't work for you, move on to the next or try elements of each. Stick to a particular method once you have found it.

Zen has a section to itself. This Japanese form of meditation is one of the most difficult to master – but can be enormously rewarding. Study its methods carefully, but don't push yourself. If it appeals to you, you may find it useful to find a Zen teacher who will give you detailed instruction and guidance.

At very advanced stages of meditation, highly spiritual experiences can occur. The last chapter of this book explains some of these phenomena and will guide you on how best to prepare your body and mind to receive this level of spirituality. However, occurrences such as out-of-body experiences and hallucinations are rare, and, for the most part, occur only in meditators who have devoted much of their lives to the search for enlightenment. It is important to understand the nature of these states so that we can become more receptive, but be patient – such spirituality takes years (perhaps a lifetime) of practice.

THE GATEWAY

An old Zen Buddhist text tells us that if we wish to learn to meditate we must first pass through the "gateless gate". Like most of the paradoxical sayings associated with Zen, this apparent riddle conveys a profound and inescapable truth. For although the gate is real enough, it is at the same time illusory, being nothing more than the inner mental chatter that keeps us from the deeper level of our minds.

A Path
Without End

When beginning meditation, one common mistake is to have a definite goal in mind, and to pursue it doggedly. We might decide to meditate to combat stress, to experience blissful states, or even to become enlightened, but these aims only set up "gateless gates" that impede progress. By suggesting that we know where meditation will lead, we create fixed concepts about it, which obscure the actual experience. The best approach is one of a relaxed "not knowing" and total open-mindedness. So we can believe in the benefits of meditation, but should avoid having fixed ideas about how these will arise and what they will feel like. In this sense, meditation is a path without end. We have expectations that attract us to it in the first place, but once practice begins these must be put aside, and meditation entered into as an experience complete in itself.

Commentators have sometimes referred to meditation as a journey into vastness, or, as Zen Master Dogen described it, "just sitting". This means a total absorption in the practice of meditation itself, without intention or expectation, and without impatience or disappointment.

What is Meditation?

Put simply, meditation is the experience of the limitless nature of the mind when it ceases to be dominated by its usual mental chatter. Think for a moment of the sky. If the sky is continually covered by clouds, we are never able to see its true nature. Roll the clouds away, and magically we experience the blue vastness of the sky in all its beauty. If the mind is continually clouded by thoughts, we are never able to experience it in and of itself. All that we experience is the cloud-cover of its contents.

Why should we want to experience the mind in and of itself? The answer is that it represents our true nature, a nature that is naturally calm and serene, unclouded by the various anxieties and wishes, hopes and fears that usually occupy our attention. To experience the mind in this unclouded way is to experience the sense of being fully and vitally alive, yet at the same time deeply at peace within ourselves.

Meditation brings with it many other benefits for body and mind, but all of these depend upon the ability to experience this central state of alert yet peaceful being.

A way of understanding this is to imagine the mind as a pool of water that for years we have been busily churning into mud with our mental chatter. Once the churning stops, the mud settles to the bottom, and the pool becomes clear. Not only can we now see the limpid, pure water itself, but also we can enjoy other pleasures, such as quenching our thirst, and bathing. Its clarity and cleanliness allow us to see through to the bottom of the pool, and discover there a new world of interest and wonder. When the mind becomes calm and still in meditation, we come to a much deeper understanding of ourselves and of our own true nature.

By stilling and calming the

thoughts, meditation also stills and calms the emotions. Thought and emotion are inextricably linked in our everyday lives. The mind goes over painful memories, current worries and concerns for the future, and as it does so it sparks off emotions such as regret, anger and fear. When the mind enters into meditation, the emotions experience a new sense of peace. Even if troubling thoughts arise, much of their usual power is lacking. The meditator is able to observe them objectively, without becoming lost in them and identifying with them. As a result, his or her ability to rouse unwelcome emotions decreases. At the centre of everything, the tranquillity of mind and feeling remains. Potentially disturbing thoughts pass through the mind like clouds across the face of the sun, and are replaced by an equanimity only possible when one is at peace with oneself.

Meditation should never be thought of as an external technique that we impose upon ourselves, much as we might learn a foreign language or master a computer. It is in essence a re-discovery of something that has always been within us, an opening of half-familiar pages in a book that we once loved but have put aside. This does not mean that in meditation we return to the mind of a child. Meditation does not ask us to relinquish our life experiences nor to distrust the power of thought. It also does not ask us to become different or less interesting people than we are now. Once the meditation session is over, the mind returns to the plans and concerns that are its usual way of being – but now with an added clarity and power in its thinking, and a greater ability to meet both the challenges and the frustrations with which life continually confronts us.

Meditation does not take us away from the world, but helps us to become more clear-sighted and effective people within it. It also enables us to become more sensitive and compassionate toward other people and toward the natural world, because it develops within us a sense of the unity and inter-dependence of all things, and an awareness of what it means to be human. With this greater sensitivity and awareness comes an enhanced feeling of self-awareness and self-acceptance. For the first time, we really sense the deep mystery and the precious nature of life.

Levels of Thought

One of the first goals of meditation is to still and calm random thoughts. In order to achieve this, it is helpful to identify four different levels of thinking. The first and lowest level is *negative thought*, which includes feelings of anger, fear, sadness, regret and unease. Negative thought makes us egotistical and lazy. The second level is *wasteful thought*, when we waste our time worrying about things that might not happen, or about things that are outside our control. The third level is *necessary thought*, such as "I must not forget to pay the electricity bill", or "I must remember to send a birthday card". The highest level is *positive thought*, which encourages peace, harmony, creativity, love and happiness. In meditation we can free our minds from negative and wasteful thoughts and elevate them to the highest level.

The Meditative Custom

Christianity, Buddhism, Hinduism, Islam, Judaism, Taoism, Shinto, Jainism and the shamanistic and pagan traditions have all taught adherents how to turn their minds inward in order to plumb its mysteries and develop a relationship with the source from which our thoughts arise. The practice of meditation – and of contemplation and prayer – lies at the heart of the great spiritual traditions.

Although we may refer to these traditions as spiritual, they are also practical psychologies for exploring and training the mind, and in many cases they are systems of philosophy and of physical culture as well. Only in recent Western history have these various categories become separated from each other, to the detriment of each of them. And only in recent Western history has the importance of meditation been virtually ignored, requiring us to turn eastward to rediscover those techniques that were once as familiar in the West as they have always been in the East. Such a need to turn eastward means that particular reference is made to Hindu and Buddhist meditative practices (see pp.90–9). But this does not imply a doctrinal approach, as meditation is for those who follow all traditions – or those who follow no tradition at all (it does not require allegiance to any particular faith or creed).

In fact, the more we study the great traditions, the more we recognize that there are many underlying

The soul who meditates on the Self is content to serve the Self and rests satisfied within the Self; there remains nothing more to accomplish.

Bhagavad Gita (c.200BCE)

similarities. It is a strange quirk of human nature that people look for differences and divisions between things (which leads to conflict) rather than for similarities and agreements (which leads to balance and harmony). Nowhere is this more evident than in the field of ideas and beliefs and of psychological and spiritual practices. In meditation, all of the great traditions teach the same fundamental steps. The details may vary, but the bedrock is the same.

The very antiquity and durability of the great traditions provides testament to their efficacy in helping people to live successful lives. The founders of two of these traditions, Christ and the Buddha, lived respectively 2,000 and 2,500 years ago. The Hindu *rishis*, responsible for the *Vedas* (some of the oldest books in the world), lived in India around 4,000 years ago. Around the same time, the ancient Egyptians depicted people sitting in what appear to be straight-backed meditative poses.

The first book of the Hebrew Bible was probably written in the 5th century BCE, but dates back to a much earlier oral tradition; the Koran was written down in the 7th century CE; and the *Tao Te Ching* probably dates from the 4th century BCE.

The Western Meditative Tradition

In the West, the meditative tradition has been particularly strong in both the Russian and Greek Orthodox Churches. St Basil wrote in the 4th century CE that "When the mind is still and not dissipated through the world by external things it returns to itself, and by means of itself ascends to the thought of God." The technique that was most frequently used in the Orthodox Churches was the repetition of the Jesus Prayer ("Lord Jesus Christ, Son of God, have mercy on me a sinner"). This is a form of mantra meditation (see *Mantras*, pp.123–5), and its transformative effect is beautifully chronicled in two classic texts, *The Way of the Pilgrim* (1942) and *The Pilgrim Continues His Way* (1943), both of which have been translated into English by R. M. French.

The First Steps

People come to meditation for a variety of reasons and from a range of backgrounds. However, they often share the same misconception, namely that meditation can be mastered simply by reading about it and memorizing the various techniques, in much the same way that they mastered subjects at school. Few beliefs could be more misleading. You could become the world's foremost expert on the history and nature of every meditation technique ever developed, yet remain a complete novice at using the techniques themselves. This is because learning to meditate depends first and foremost upon direct experience. Teachers and books can set you on the right path, and help you to negotiate any pitfalls you may encounter, but their instruction is no substitute for what you learn from the personal act of meditation.

This being the case, what is the first step? When asked this question by a student, a Zen master picked up a stick and wrote in the dust on the ground the symbol that means "attention". "But surely there must be more to it than that?" the student persisted. The master picked up the stick again and wrote "attention" once more. "But what else?" came the plea. A third time the master took up the stick and wrote on the ground "attention". Attention – attention – attention.

A relaxed, focused concentration upon a chosen stimulus, attention is

By meditation upon light and upon radiance, knowledge of the spirit can be reached and peace can be achieved.

Patanjali (c.300BCE)

the underlying key to all meditation, no matter which particular technique we decide to adopt. Without this concentration there is no meditation. Whenever our minds are fully attentive in this way to one particular stimulus, with no random thoughts distracting us, we are entering into meditation. This means, in effect, that meditation can be done at any time and in any place, and not simply when we are sitting on a meditation cushion in a calm and peaceful room. We can meditate on a train, when we are waiting for a bus, walking in the middle of a crowd, or engaged in virtually any activity when it is safe to turn the mind inward. We can even meditate by focusing fully upon the activity itself, rather than allowing the mind, as usually happens, to wander off on its own. Thus no matter how mundane the task, if we absorb ourselves fully in it, with the concentration that a small child places in a toy, then we can say that we are meditating.

In reality, however, it is extremely difficult to build up concentration of this kind without regular sessions in the peace of a still, quiet room. Only with constant practice does the mind begin to learn how to focus. After all, we have spent most of our lives training our minds to juggle thoughts and think of many things at once — work, home, family and friends. Inevitably, it will take a certain amount of time and application to remedy this.

Some people may fear that if they develop this ability to focus and calm the mind it may be to the detriment of their powers of thinking. They need have no such fear — the exact opposite is the case. When the mind returns to thinking after a session of meditation, it is with greater clarity and renewed mental energy. In fact, meditation can actually be used to enable us to watch our thinking, like a detached observer, and to recognize the tricks that the untrained mind habitually plays to distract us from what we are doing by setting off an irrelevant train of thought, or by recalling memories, arousing emotions or diverting us into fantasies and daydreams. One of the first steps toward focusing attention is simply to sit quietly and still the body, and then to become aware of distracting thoughts.

Stilling the Body

Exercise 1

This exercise is designed to teach you how to sit quietly and still so that you can focus your attention. By watching our thoughts and learning to identify distractions, we begin the path of meditation.

1. Wear loose, comfortable clothes so that your movements are not restricted. Find a quiet place where you will not be disturbed – perhaps your bedroom or a peaceful spot in the garden.

2. Sit comfortably on the ground, with your legs stretched out. Close your eyes and concentrate on relaxing each part of your legs, beginning with your hips and finishing by stretching and relaxing your feet. If you feel comfortable doing so, bring your legs in toward your body so that you are sitting cross-legged.

3. Turn your attention inward and be aware of the thoughts and emotions that arise. Are you at ease or a little self-conscious? Do you notice any emotions or a change of mood? Is there a sense of excitement or are you bored? Is your head filled with distracting thoughts? None of these reactions is right or wrong. For the moment, just be aware of them.

Physical Benefits

Many physical benefits can result from the regular practice of meditation, including relief from insomnia, reduced blood pressure, improvement in posture, increased energy, greater pain management and enhanced (and greater control over) libido. None of these benefits can be guaranteed, but in many cases it does seem that by deeply relaxing and calming the nervous system, meditation allows the body to function more efficiently, to improve its ability to heal itself, and to return to a healthier and more natural state. Many yoga exercises (grounded, among others, in the Hindu and the Taoist traditions) further enhance these benefits, but meditation can also be extremely effective by itself.

To experience physical benefits from meditation, you should use the meditative state to help increase body awareness, as described in *Exercise 2, Preparing the Body* (p.26) and *Exercise 11, Harmony of the Self* (p.71).

From early childhood onward, most of us get into bad habits in the way we use our bodies. These eventually include not only a bad diet, excessive drinking, smoking and lack of exercise, but also the way in which we hold ourselves, the way we move, and the way we breathe. Over the years tensions creep up on us almost unnoticed; our breathing becomes irregular and shallow, our posture slumps, we sit badly, we walk badly and stand badly, and we even use our voices badly.

Meditation allows us not only to look at what is going on in our minds, but also at what is going on in our bodies. It gives us the space to check up on ourselves, to become re-acquainted with how it feels to live within our bodies, to become conscious of the way that we breathe, and of the many minor aches and pains to which we subject ourselves by our usual way of being, so that we can at first consciously, but then with practice unconsciously, counteract them.

This improvement in body awareness should not just be confined to your sessions of sitting meditation. Develop the habit, right from the start of your meditative journey, of rising unhurriedly from your cushion or chair when your meditation session is over. Try to walk in the same relaxed and unhurried way, with continuing awareness of your body and how it feels.

At first this heightened awareness may last for only a few minutes, but with practice it will flow through more of your waking hours, not intrusively but as a background to whatever else you are doing.

Help the process by trying to return to full body awareness as often as possible during the day, particularly when you are in a stressful situation of some kind. Notice how imperceptibly but comprehensively your body tightens up, putting unnecessary strain on muscles, joints and ligaments. Then notice how grateful your body feels as you relax and let go of this tightness by focusing and relaxing each body part.

see exercise overleaf

Preparing the Body

Exercise 2

In the exercise below you will learn to relax each part of your body in preparation for meditation.

1. Sit comfortably and allow your concentration to rest upon your right foot. Wiggling your toes can help you to focus on this area. (Start with your left side if you are left-handed.)

2. Now relax your foot and allow your attention to move to your right calf. Is there any tension there? If so, let it go by tensing the muscles and then freeing them.

3. Now move your awareness up to your right thigh, then your buttock, then the abdomen, then your chest, then down your right arm to your hand and back again to your shoulder, then to the muscles of your face, and finally to the crown of your head. Be aware in each case of any tension, and let it go. How does each part of your body feel? Be aware of both the sensation on the skin and deeper sensations in the muscles and ligaments themselves.

4. Now continue the process by moving down to the neck, the left shoulder, the left arm, the back, and down the left leg to the foot.

Mind Benefits

The term *mind* covers three levels of our mental life. These are the conscious level (the thoughts, feelings and emotions of which we are currently aware); the preconscious (everything that we can call into consciousness at will); and the unconscious (the vast reservoir of memories, unacknowledged wishes and fears that lie below normal awareness, but that can exert a major influence over how we think and behave). Many of the great traditions, together with some newer psychotherapeutic movements in the West, maintain that spiritual and psychological development depend in part upon improving communication between the conscious and unconscious levels of the mind. Such communication not only enhances our self-knowledge and self-understanding, but also provides access to the creative and transformative abilities that often lie latent within each of us.

Meditation can be one of the most effective ways of improving this communication. When the conscious level of the mind becomes still, awareness of the deeper, unconscious, level grows. The unconscious is an essential part of ourselves: it determines many of our hopes, anxieties, likes and dislikes, and other important personal characteristics, and perhaps contains the secrets of our very being (see *Exercise 4, Who Am I?*, p.31). Failure to access the unconscious means that we remain stranger to an essential part of our own nature. The Russian mystic Georgei Guridieff likened the mind to a house, and suggested that our failure to explore its deeper levels is like living in a single room instead of roving through the spacious corridors from one room to another.

The principal mind benefits of meditation are improved tranquillity, patience, concentration and memory, and enhanced understanding and sympathy toward others.

Tranquillity arises naturally from the alert state of peaceful being that is central to meditation. In this state the meditator is in the role of an observer, conscious of whatever arises in the mind, but detached from it, instead of identified with it. Thoughts, emotions, feelings and memories are seen without judgment and allowed to pass into and out of awareness like images across a screen. Essentially, when we meditate we become aware that although we have these thoughts and feelings, they are not who we are. They are impermanent, transitory events in our mental life, whose power over us is in direct proportion to the strength of our attachment or aversion toward them. True identity lies beyond such passing experiences. This does not mean that the meditator becomes insensitive to pleasure and pain; it means only that pleasure and pain no longer take control.

Patience comes as a consequence of the unhurried act of peaceful sitting, and the contrast it provides to the frantic pace at which most of us normally live our lives. The meditator becomes aware of the essential "nowness" of existence. All we have is the instant of each present moment. Concern for the future and over-preoccupation with the past are seen as artificial distractions from the direct experience of living. Something of this unhurried approach persists even when we are not meditating, so that life comes to be experienced at a gentler pace, and its minor irritations are faced with greater equanimity. The result is not only reduced stress for ourselves and often for others, but clearer vision and more objective judgment. Hurry is seen as counter-productive, and with patience there comes a greater ability to discriminate between what is important and what is not.

Concentration permits the meditator to practise mindfulness. The usually scattered elements of the attention are drawn together and focused, clearly and calmly, upon a single stimulus, initially our breathing. Whenever

28

Watching the Thoughts

Exercise 3

An early exercise in meditation is to take an objective look at the mind in order to see what goes on within it, and the tricks that it can play.

1. Sit and relax. Close your eyes and turn your attention inward. As objectively as you can, watch the thoughts that pass through your awareness. Don't judge them, or attempt to hang on to pleasant ones, or push unpleasant ones away. Just watch.

2. Notice the nature and content of your thoughts — how one thought leads to another, and how quickly a chain of associations is set up. Notice how these associations sometimes follow a single theme, or go off at a tangent into a quite different set of considerations. Notice how intent your mind seems on distracting your attention, and observe the strategies it uses to do so.

3. Notice how easily your objective awareness does in fact disappear, and you become "lost" in your thoughts. Each time this happens, gently re-establish awareness.

4. Continue the exercise for as long as seems comfortable. Afterward, write down what you have discovered about your mind.

the mind wanders, it is brought gently back to this point of focus. By degrees, as the mind becomes concentrated, it calms down and becomes tranquil.

Memory is the fourth key mind benefit. Much of our inability to remember things stems from our failure to attend properly to them in the first place. Often our minds are busily thinking about something quite different, with the result that we function practically as automatons. Worse still, we frequently tend to do several things at once without concentrating properly on any of them. Meditation trains the mind to be in the present moment, focused upon whatever is at the centre of awareness. The result is that more of what we experience is registered and transferred to our memory stores. Together with the practice of mindfulness (see pp.32–3), meditation helps us to use our minds in a more efficient way.

Enhanced understanding and sympathy toward others is based in part on enhanced understanding and sympathy toward ourselves. With meditation comes increased self-

insight and understanding, and a corresponding increase in our understanding of other people. We become aware that what we see inside ourselves is also there in them. Other people have the same emotions and feelings as ourselves. They make the same mistakes, seek the same goals, and can show the same compassion and generosity. Even if we consider that there is no need for their anger or for their fears, we can appreciate the reality of the suffering that these emotions cause them.

For the advanced meditator, there often comes an awareness of the underlying unity and interdependence of all things. This leads to a recognition that to harm others is to harm oneself, and that to show kindness to others is to show kindness to oneself. The weaknesses and vulnerabilities of other people thus come to be seen as images of our own weaknesses and vulnerabilities. There is a growing awareness of shared humanity, which leads naturally to the development of what in the East is called *ahimsa*, an emphasis upon non-violence and a concern and respect for all life.

Who Am I?

Exercise 4

The question "Who am I?" is one that we will keep in mind throughout this book. For the moment, the spirit of inquiry, rather than the answers, is what matters. We have stumbled upon a puzzle that intrigues and engages us, but which we do not expect to solve just yet. For the time being, we are content to watch, ask and wait.

1. Sit comfortably and relax by tensing and releasing your muscles. Take a deep breath and slowly exhale, imagining that any remaining tension is set free with your out-breath. Close your eyes and turn your attention inward.

2. Watch the thoughts that pass through your awareness, but don't judge them. Try not to hang on to pleasant thoughts, or to push unpleasant ones away. Just watch.

3. Now go one step further and ask yourself "Who is it who is watching?"

4. Repeat the question mentally from time to time throughout the meditation, but always in a light, half-amused way, without demanding an answer.

Mindfulness

 Mindfulness means putting the mind fully into the present, so that we are always engaged with what we are doing. The Buddha spoke of the four foundations of mindfulness as being mindfulness of the body (awareness of the body's movements); mindfulness of the feelings (awareness of bodily sensations); mindfulness of the mental states (awareness of moods, emotions, attitudes and our mental disposition); and mindfulness of mental objects (awareness of what we are thinking and observing). Mindfulness can therefore be thought of as a process of self-monitoring, of the attention to which we referred in *The First Steps* (pp.21–2). It should flow continuously throughout our waking life, so that meditation is not confined to our sessions of sitting, but rather becomes a way of being. In practice, this is difficult for all except very advanced meditators, but short

Awaken!

The Russian mystic Georgei Guridieff frequently pointed out that much of human misery is caused by the fact that we live our lives mechanically, never properly attending to what it is to be alive. Contemporary American psychologist Charles Tart describes us as being in a kind of "consensus trance". These teachers, and all the great traditions, refer constantly to the need to awaken. This acute sense of being properly awake is really another word for mindfulness. Tart suggests that the concept of mindfulness should be motivated by the assertion, "I want to know what really is, regardless of how I prefer things to be." Our lack of mindfulness insulates us from the direct experience of what this mysterious, intriguing, maddening thing called life actually is.

sessions of this intensive work are helpful for the beginner. These can take place at odd moments, but it is better to schedule them for times of the day when distractions are unlikely to occur.

During these sessions, ask yourself four questions: "What am I doing now?"; "What are my physical sensations now?"; "What is my mental state now?"; "What am I thinking or seeing or hearing now?". Alternatively, keep a running commentary of each of your movements and mind states. For example, "Now I am walking toward the window — now I am looking out at the garden and watching the flowers in the breeze — I am feeling happy — now I am turning away from the window and walking toward the table — now I feel a slight pain in my left knee — now I am remembering tripping on the pavement when I was on holiday last summer."

One of the immediate benefits of this practice is an improvement in memory. By focusing upon what we are doing when we are actually doing it, we eliminate annoying experiences such as failing to recall where we have put something only a few minutes ago.

Watching the Emotions

In explaining what meditation is, we said that thoughts and emotions are closely connected, and that meditation can help us with the latter as well as with the former. We spend a lot of time in combat with our emotions, trying either to suppress them or to prevent them from being apparent, and they influence our effectiveness as agents acting upon our own lives and the world at large. Emotions come and go just as thoughts come and go, but we are not our emotions, just as we are not our thoughts.

When we look closely at what happens in our inner lives, we observe that when we remember or anticipate an unpleasant experience, we feel anxiety; when we remember or anticipate a pleasant experience, we feel happiness and excitement. Similarly, when we think of a difficult colleague or acquaintance, we may feel anger, hostility or resentment; when we think of a partner or our children, we feel love; when we think of those who

are suffering, we feel sympathy and compassion. By virtue of this close connection, the practice of distancing ourselves from our thoughts in meditation means that we are also able to distance ourselves from our emotions. Naturally, there is no need to distance ourselves from positive emotions, such as love, happiness and compassion, and there are meditations that help us to develop such welcome feelings. But meditation leaves us less at the mercy of our emotions, and less likely to be disturbed by those that upset us or distract us from the focused tranquillity of meditation itself.

However, unwanted thoughts inevitably still arise from time to time, together with their attendant emotions — particularly in the early stages of meditation practice. Alternatively, the process may sometimes appear to be reversed, with emotions appearing to arise unbidden, and then to trigger off associated thoughts. When such negative emotions arise, they should

be treated in the same way that we treat intrusive thoughts — that is, they are to be observed as transitory events with which we should refrain from identifying.

In the case of stubborn emotions that in spite of our attempts to banish them refuse to disappear, meditation can be used to look into their nature. The emotion concerned may, for example, be fear — in which case the meditator asks what exactly is this thing called fear that I am feeling? Is it a physical sensation? If so, what kind of sensation is it, and where is it located? I recognize it as unpleasant, in which case what is it that makes it unpleasant? Is it the physical sensation itself, or is it my reaction to the physical sensation? If it is my reaction, what is the nature of this reaction? In spite of myself, am I secretly rather keen to hang on to my fear? If so, what is the reason for this desire to hang on? Do I see the emotion as part of my identity? Do I recognize myself in the emotion? Am I afraid that if I let go of the emotion I will feel less alive?

This practice of looking into the real nature of emotions

sounds much more difficult than it really is. It involves simply looking and seeing what is there, without blaming yourself for how you are, and without struggling against the emotion. The calmer you are in your attitude toward a stubborn emotion, the sooner it will pass and you will relax again.

Pleasant emotions feel very different from unpleasant ones, but even they can exert too much control over us, prompting disappointment when they fail to find fulfilment as we might have expected. Enjoyable as they are, pleasant emotions can become addictive, so we should learn to look gently at them, keeping them in perspective, assessing how superficial or transient they may actually be. Their tendency to come and go illustrates how important it is that we try not to define ourselves by them, just as we should not identify with negative emotions and thoughts.

Paradoxically, the pursuit of pleasant emotions often makes them much more difficult to find, so we should try not to mark them as a goal for meditation. Pleasant emotions are there to be savoured, but they are certainly not the end of our meditative journey.

Making Friends with Negative Emotions

Our emotions are often more out of control than our thoughts. We may know we have no reason to feel depressed, or that an angry response is exactly what an antagonist wants to provoke in us, yet we cannot prevent the emotion from arising. We may even know that no one can *make* us feel anything against our will. Ultimately, we are responsible for our own unwanted feelings. Yet we still cannot free ourselves from them. If we struggle against our negative emotions, we only seem to strengthen them. In Buddhist teaching it is said that we should "make friends" with our negative emotions: that is, we should cease to fear them. We can then observe them calmly and go on to explore what it is in ourselves that is irritated, for example, by someone's inefficiency, or upset by their criticism.

Pitfalls in Meditation

It has already been stressed that meditation does not adversely affect our powers of thinking. On the contrary, the clarity and enhanced concentration that it produces helps the mind to work more effectively at all levels. You can also be reassured that meditation need not make you "blissed out", or removed from the real world and indifferent to the concerns of everyday life. Certainly it adds a new dimension of awareness to our way of seeing ourselves and the world, but it risks distracting us from normal living only if we devote our meditation exclusively to the experience of tranquillity. Important though tranquillity is in meditation, it is a essentially a stepping-stone to insight, by which the mind not only enjoys the clarity that meditation brings, but also uses this clarity to see into deeper levels of being.

However, from time to time during meditation experiences arise that could cause alarm. Temporary side-effects or discomforting sensations are a not uncommon result of meditation. You may, for example, feel unaccountably heavy, as though you are sinking down through the floor; or you may feel quite the opposite – weightless, as if floating away. You may lose the sense of feeling in your legs, or in other parts of your body; or you may experience feelings of tingling or pulsations coursing through your body or over the top of your head.

Some meditators may perspire profusely, shiver, or find that they are trembling. Their hearts pound, or they breathe rapidly. Conversely, breathing may become so gentle that it seems to have stopped altogether. Occasionally there may be visions or hallucinations: these are usually pleasant, but sometimes they may seem to be threatening. Experiences of this kind usually occur only to advanced practitioners, but they are not unknown to beginners.

The advisable way to deal with these minor physical problems is to observe the phenomena with the same detachment as you observe your thoughts and emotions. They are simply creations of the mind and, provided that the meditator remains calm and relaxed, they will soon dissolve into the same space as all other mental creations. Some experiences – in particular beautiful visions or abstract forms and colours – are in fact a welcome sign of progress, indicating contact with deeper, creative levels of consciousness. However, as with the experience of tranquillity, it is important not to become attached to these visions (see *Exercise 5, Eliminating Discomforts*, opposite). Attachment causes two problems: the meditator may strive consciously to re-experience the visions, and then be frustrated when they fail to arise; or, if the visions continue to come readily, he or she may become distracted by their beauty instead of moving deeper into the meditation practice itself.

Most of the great meditation traditions teach that meditators sometimes find themselves gaining powers of extrasensory perception at a certain stage in their practice. These should not be allowed to become an end in themselves.

Another potential pitfall is that meditation may affect social relationships – for example, if one partner becomes a serious practitioner while the other shows no interest. Meditation does make us more concerned with the fundamental issues in life, and some friends and family may find this unsettling. But issues of this kind are a feature of all personal growth work – even of the normal processes of change and development that occur as we grow older. The best advice is that meditators must understand and be sympathetic toward the concerns of those close to them. The enhanced sensitivity that comes with meditation is a help in this, in that it allows us to be tolerant and understanding of the hopes and fears of others.

Eliminating Discomforts

Exercise 5

This exercise is designed to help you eliminate physical discomforts and other experiences that distract you during your meditation. These should be observed with detachment as when you observe your thoughts.

1. Close your eyes and sit as still as you can.

2. After a short while, you may become aware of discomforting sensations and experience an urge to change your position. Allow yourself to move and then sit still again.

3. When you next begin to feel discomfort, sit through the urge. Notice that it is possible to resist such distractions. Be aware of the restlessness of your mind, and of the way in which this restlessness is reflected in physical movement.

4. As you continue to sit, you may experience distracting visions or hallucinations. As with physical discomforts, do not allow yourself to become attached to these experiences — let them pass through your mind and float away. If they refuse to disappear, observe them as objectively as you would any other thought. Ask yourself "Who is it who has these experiences?"

Entrances

You are now ready to pass through the gateless gate of meditation and start your practice in earnest. You understand what meditation is, you know some of its benefits and the possible pitfalls, you know the techniques for watching thoughts and emotions, you are aware of the importance of mindfulness, and you have been introduced to the question implicit in meditation, "Who am I?"

Entering the gateless gate requires a certain amount of self-discipline and commitment. You may be tempted to give up in the face of initial failure to quieten mental chatter, although it is precisely because our minds are so busy that we need to meditate. Perhaps, after initial success, your mind wants to revert to its original wayward habits. Such setbacks must be met with patience — they happen to us all.

Even if your initial results seem excellent, you may be tempted to discontinue the practice on the grounds that it has completed its work. But meditation is a way of life — a path without end.

Overcome the temptation to give up too soon. Make an initial commitment to practise every day for at least a month. And make an equal commitment to treat your meditation practice with respect and patience.

The Setting

The importance of being able to meditate anywhere and in any physical position has already been stressed. But the ability to do this should not be regarded as an alternative to regular sessions of sitting meditation, as it is precisely these sessions that strengthen your practice to the point where you can return to the meditative state whenever you wish.

Give some thought to the setting for your regular sessions. A room kept exclusively for meditation is the ideal, but few of us can afford such luxury. It may not even be possible to meditate always in the same room. But if you can, choose a room that has peaceful associations for you, such as your bedroom, or perhaps a summer room or conservatory. Whichever room you choose, it should be one in which you will feel comfortable for stretches of time,

and one where you are least likely to be disturbed. Avoid cluttered or untidy rooms.

The colour of your meditation room is important – ideally, the room should match the state of mind of the meditator. Many people find that restful colours, such as blue and green, help put them in a peaceful frame of mind – traditionally, for example, the "green room" is where actors go to calm their nerves and collect their thoughts before a performance. In Tibetan Buddhism, however, the meditation hall is predominantly red. Usually thought of as an arousing colour, red may help the meditator to stay watchful and alert. In the West, purple and mauve are often regarded as particularly spiritual colours; while orange and saffron are preferred in the East. Many meditators choose white because it is a cool, pure and undistracting colour.

Whatever your preference, try not to choose a room with a busy patterned wallpaper, or anything else likely to distract your attention. If all else fails, a curtain or cloth draped over the wall in front of you is often

the answer — some people like to beautify it with natural objects such as leaves or flowers.

Try to create a mini-environment around you that can, if necessary, be carried from place to place. This may consist only of your meditation cushion or stool, and the clothes and any adornments you keep specially for meditation (see pp.52–3). However, you may wish to include incense and an incense burner, seasonal flowers, floating candles in an attractive water-filled bowl, or a small low folding table (useful for holding pictures, books or any ritual objects). You may also like to have a favourite tape or CD playing — music

can be useful to settle the mind. However, you should dispense with music as your practice of meditation deepens, as its very beauty can distract you from self-exploration — and can lull you into a sleepy, trance-like state, which is pleasant in itself but definitely not the state of meditation. It is important that you should not become over-reliant on any of these aids, or you will find meditation difficult without them. All you really need in order to meditate is your own mind.

As far as is possible, avoid the risk of interruptions during the session: this is particularly difficult if small children are around, and unfair on the children — it is better to wait until they are safely in bed. Disconnect the telephone if you are on your own; if there are other people in the house, ask them not to disturb you. Whatever the setting, sounds from the street or from neighbours are often unavoidable, and it is a mistake to try too hard to shut these out of your mind. They are part of the experience of the moment, and should simply be observed and let go like anything else that comes into your awareness. Imagine that each disturbing sound is a bird that you are holding in your hand — let it go and as you visualize it flying away up into the sky, allow the sound to filter out of your mind.

Try to avoid anger or resentment toward those who cause a disturbance. Strong feelings of this kind cause far more interference to your meditation than the noises themselves. Also, try not to allow the noises to set off a train of distracting thoughts, such as attempts to identify them or their place of origin. Before you are aware of it, you are likely to become lost in these trains of thought, to the detriment of your powers of concentration.

The Support and Understanding of Others

Other members of your household may disturb you or cause difficulties while you are meditating. This could be because they fear that meditation will change you in some unwelcome way; or they may resent the quiet moments that you have to yourself. If this happens, encourage them to join you: meditating together, with shared motivation and patience, is potentially very beneficial. However, if they remain unenthusiastic about meditating with you, do not press them. When they see the benefical effects on you, they may very well change their minds. Whatever the situation, emphasize that meditation helps to make someone closer rather than more remote from others, and that it should improve the meditator's spirits and health, which benefits everyone.

Improvised Meditation

Exercise 6

Even in the early stages it is valuable to practise meditation at times other than your daily sessions. Choose occasions when it is safe and convenient to do so. Pick a focus for concentration and fix your awareness upon it.

1. Sit comfortably and relax.

2. Select a sound (such as birdsong) and concentrate your attention on it. Each time your attention tries to wander, bring it gently back to the sound.

3. Each time your mind tries to label the sound, or to use it to set up a train of associations, bring it back to direct contemplation of the sound itself. Centre your attention on hearing.

4. Repeat the exercise, this time by viewing an object (the more familiar the better, animate or inanimate). Concentrate your attention, blinking only when necessary. Become aware of it as occupying space, without a name and without a function other than to be itself. Do not think of it in terms of colour, of beauty (or lack of it) or of context. Centre your attention on the pure fact of seeing.

Time and Duration

Many people find that the three times most suitable for a daily meditation session are first thing in the morning, midday and late evening. Research suggests that about 70 percent of meditators favour the morning, 25 percent prefer the evening and only a handful choose midday. Your choice may depend not only on convenience, but also on your own individual 24-hour biorhythm (a recurring cycle of biological processes that affect your emotional, intellectual and physical activity), and on the regular pattern of your day. In addition, some people find that their mind quietens more easily at certain times of the day than at others.

If possible, it is helpful to meditate in both the morning and the evening, but in a busy life this is often not practicable. The advantage of morning meditation is that your mind is often at its calmest after a good night's sleep, while the advantage of evening meditation is that it gives your mind the perfect opportunity to calm down and re-balance after the day's activities. Meditating at midday provides a short period of recuperation and rest between the two halves of the working day. It is good to experiment, not only to see which time suits you best, but also to note if there are any differences in the texture of your meditative experience over the waking hours. The benefit of meditating at the same time each day is that it becomes an established feature of daily life, like eating a meal. In a short while you will find that when the time for daily meditation approaches, your mind turns of its own accord to the practice. However, you should take care not to let your meditation become too routine – a habit that is almost as bad as not meditating at all.

The longer the duration of your meditation sessions, the better your progress is likely to be. However, it is a mistake to be too ambitious.

Ten minutes (or even five) is a good beginning. You can then either allow the time to expand of its own accord, or decide that you will increase the duration by a set number of minutes each week (even as little as one or two). Aim eventually for a minimum of half an hour each day (in two periods of 15 minutes each if you prefer).

Advanced meditators usually sit for at least an hour a day, and perhaps devote one day a month to eight or more half-hour sessions, with silent periods in between. Or they may periodically attend a retreat for even more intensive practice (see pp.83–4).

Vacations, or the presence of visitors, can interrupt your schedule, and once you break the rhythm, it is often difficult to re-establish. In these circumstances, try to do at least a few minutes of meditation each day whatever the surroundings. This may be just a brief session on the beach or in a garden, but it will help to maintain your practice. On many of these occasions, a few minutes of direct contemplation (see *Exercise 6, Improvised Meditation*, p.45) is particularly beneficial.

see exercise overleaf

Awareness of Time

Exercise 7

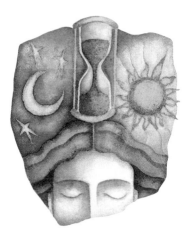

During meditation one often loses all track of time. Saints and holy men and women in all traditions have been reported as sitting in meditation sometimes for days on end. In these instances bodily metabolism appears to slow down, as if the meditator is in a state of suspended animation. To explore the phenomenon of drifting time, introduce some untimed meditation sessions into your practice quite early on, but take care not to turn them into endurance tests.

1. Note what time it is as you sit comfortably and relax.

2. Close your eyes and turn your attention inward. Empty your mind of chattering thoughts.

3. Sit for as long as you feel comfortable. After you finish, guess the time spent in meditation.

4. When you look at your watch, you may be surprised at the extent to which your guess is an underestimation. However, if your guess is correct, do not be pleased or disappointed with yourself. Everyone responds differently to meditation, particularly at the beginning.

Rituals and Objects

The prime purpose of a ritual is to encourage a particular state of mind; for example, awe, reverence, respect, devotion or compassion. During a meditation session rituals can help to settle your mind and increase your motivation to practise. In the great traditions rituals may be used to seek the help of external forces, such as the Buddhas or bodhisattvas, patron saints, or appropriate deities – in which case they can take the form of a prayer, an invocation or mantra.

At the very least, rituals build up habits that can help to sustain the regularity of your practice. As soon as the ritual begins, your mind will turn automatically toward the meditative state. If the ritual arises from spiritual beliefs, you will feel that the practice is an act of devotion in addition to its other strengths.

Various objects can be used to support your rituals. You can sound a bell, a singing bowl or a *tinsha* (small Tibetan cymbals) at the beginning and end of the session;

you can light a stick of incense or warm some essential oil to release an aroma; you can light a single candle or float candles in a bowl; you can use a music tape (which preferably should be faded out before you start the meditation); you can read a suitable text, such as a passage from the Bible, the Koran, the Buddhist sutras, or a Hindu text such as the *Bhagavad Gita*; you can put on clothes kept for the occasion; you can gaze at a picture or a mandala (see p.108) or at a sacred symbol, such as the cross, crescent or circle.

The ritual itself may be one that already exists in your own tradition, or one that is given to you by a meditation teacher, or it may be one that you construct for yourself. The golden rule is to keep it simple – elaborate rituals are difficult to remember and time-consuming. Ensure that each part of the ritual carries meaning of some kind. This may be associated with one or other of the great teachers from within your preferred spiritual tradition.

If you have no such tradition, it may be associated with nature, or with attributes such as universal love, harmony or peace. For example, you may decide to express your gratitude for the gift of life, and then to bow to each of the four directions in turn and wish peace and love to all other beings.

Whatever the ritual happens to be, allow yourself a few sessions in which to experiment and get it right, then stick to it and carry it out sincerely and with awareness. Constantly changing the ritual, like constantly changing your meditation practice, will prevent your mind settling into the routine that is so important to meditation practice.

The question is sometimes asked, do the external forces toward which the members of the various traditions direct their rituals really exist? The Greek gods, Hindu gods, the Buddha and bodhisattvas, Christ and the saints – are they really there in any real sense, and can they be contacted through ritual (and through meditation itself) and be asked for their help? People with great faith will immediately answer that certainly they can, but those with less faith may remain uncertain. Are there spiritual beings, and, if so, are they interested in the affairs of humans? These questions are much too profound to be answered here, and everyone must ultimately reach his or her own conclusion. One way of looking at the issue is to think of divine energy as a reservoir of infinite potential, as a primal consciousness from which all else arises (such a view is not incompatible with recent theories in modern physics). This divine energy can then be personalized through the belief systems and the creative mind of the individual. In terms of this view, Christ, the Buddha, Krishna, Shiva and the other great spiritual beings are to be thought of as existing not only in their physical forms in some distant heaven, but also as aspects of this divine energy who can manifest themselves in material form in accordance with the way in which the individual has been taught to conceptualize them.

Thus there is a very real sense in which they can be reached through ritual and prayer. In mystical experience, the mind sees beyond the manifested form and dwells in the bliss of the divine energy itself, and all the traditions teach that this state can also be achieved in the most exalted levels of meditation.

Prayer Wheels

In Tibetan Buddhism prayer wheels are favourite ritual objects. These hollow cylinders are made of wood, bone or metal, and they contain appropriate mantras or sacred texts. Some prayer wheels are small enough to be mounted on a handle and spun by a circular movement of the wrist. Other wheels are massive and are mounted in rows outside the temples where worshippers turn them as they pass by. Used at the start of meditation, a prayer wheel serves as a reminder of the need for constant mindfulness, and can become part of your ritual. Prayer flags, which flutter continually in the wind, fulfil a similar function. In mantra meditation (see pp.123–5) prayer beads (rosaries or *malas*) are frequently used, with one repetition of the mantra for each bead.

Clothes and Symbols

When choosing your clothes and adornments for the meditation session, the main consideration should be comfort. Whatever you wear must be loose enough not to distract you, and warm (or cool) enough to keep you at a comfortable temperature. Some meditators, either for comfort or in emulation of Hindu ascetics, prefer to be naked. Those who follow pagan paths may also adopt this practice, particularly if they can sit in privacy outside and thus experience what they regard as a close relationship with the natural world.

You may find wearing clothes of certain colours helps to put you in the right frame of mind for meditation. The colours that you use are largely a matter of personal choice, although white has long been a symbol of purity, blue of serenity, green of nature, and mauves and purples of spirituality. Some meditators favour the saffron colour worn by Theravadin monks, the maroon of Tibetan monks, or the brown, black or grey of other monastic orders.

It helps if you can keep at least one garment – a cloak, a prayer shawl or a blanket – exclusively for your meditation sessions. Each time you place it around your shoulders it will help turn your mind toward meditation. Certainly, it is worth changing out of everyday clothes.

Adornments are also a matter of personal preference. The Tibetan practice of hanging a prayer box (a form of locket containing a mantra, a sacred text or a symbol) around the neck is a good example. Some meditators adorn themselves with beads, or with a pendant of semi-precious stones such as lapis-lazuli (the symbol of eternal life) or amber. Christians may prefer a pectoral cross, while others often use the Egyptian *ankh* or the scarab (both of which are also symbols of eternal life). Don't be reluctant to ascribe symbolic meaning to these and other adornments. Whether these meanings are purely subjective, or

whether they carry more general significance, there is no doubt that they help your mind to turn from the concerns of daily life to the concentration and awareness of meditation. They also serve as tokens of your commitment to your practice. The fact that they have been hallowed through their use by holy men and women across the centuries can be a further incentive to practise.

The position of the hands is highly symbolic in all major Eastern traditions. These positions, or *mudras*, can be simple or intricate. In Hindu and yoga practices the hands are placed palms upward on the knees, with the thumbs and first fingers making a circle that symbolizes eternity, the absolute, and the formless realms. The *anjali mudra*, bringing the hands together as in Christian prayer, is a gesture of reverence and respect. The hands placed in the lap, right over left and with thumbs touching to make a circle (the *dhyana mudra*) is the symbol of meditation and of enlightenment, representing the higher nature triumphing over the lower and aspiring upward to the infinite, symbolized by the circle.

Postures

Being able to meditate in different positions is an important aspect of any meditative session. Do not reject the idea of meditating lying down: not only is this useful during times of sickness, but it also indicates good mind control, as it is only too easy to drift into sleep in this position.

The Jains (see p.93) often meditate standing up, feet slightly apart, arms by the sides and held just clear of the body – a difficult posture that requires great commitment. Certain traditions meditate while moving – some Sufis conduct a graceful spinning dance (see p.98), and Zen Buddhists practise a form of slow walking meditation. Tai chi and some other forms of the martial arts also combine meditation and movement. In hatha yoga adherents meditate in many different poses, including the headstand, which is said to reverse the flow of time so that you grow younger.

The most popular meditation posture is the lotus, in which you sit cross-legged with your feet up on your thighs. This is easy for those who have practised from childhood, but difficult for most people who come to it in adult life. Variants are the simpler half-lotus, in which only the foot of the upper leg is placed on the thigh, and the perfect posture (see *Exercise 8*, *Learning to Sit*, opposite), where the foot is placed on the calf.

Anyone who finds it uncomfortable to sit cross-legged should sit on an upright chair with their feet flat on the floor. In all cases, the spine should be kept straight: it is claimed that this allows energy to rise from the body up the spine toward the crown of the head where enlightenment is realized, but at the very least it helps the meditator to stay alert.

It is important to check your posture during meditation, and to correct any tendency to slump. Your head should be kept erect, with your chin held in. Your eyes can be open or closed, but for beginners closed eyes help to minimize distractions.

Learning to Sit

The seated posture is basic to meditation because it allows the body to feel balanced and to sit for long periods in relative comfort. In sitting meditation, there should be as little movement as possible – physical stillness helps mental stillness. In general, try to sit through minor aches and pains, moving only when absolutely necessary.

1. Sit cross-legged on a cushion that is thick enough to raise your bottom at least 4in (10cm) from the floor.

2. Ease forward a little so that you can bring your left heel as close to your body as possible.

3. Lift your right foot and place it on the calf of your left leg in the perfect position. (Or, if it is comfortable, place your right foot on your left thigh, in the half-lotus position.)

4. Relax your legs as much as possible. In this position, your knees should be close to the floor, but do not force them down. Each day your legs will become more supple.

Essentials

Now that your meditative journey is under way, it is useful to recall the essentials of successful meditation, to consolidate them, explore them further and progress deeper into the inner recesses of your mind.

The foundation of all meditation is the ability to focus the mind on a particular stimulus without becoming distracted by thoughts, feelings or minor physical discomforts. Through regular meditation practice the mind becomes calmer and clearer, and insight grows.

A certain level of patience and commitment is required from the meditator. Many beginners say they are useless at controlling their minds and think that meditation is not for them. But it is precisely because the mind is so wayward that we need to meditate.

To begin, commit yourself to just a few minutes of meditation each day for a month. As you progress you can gradually allow the time to lengthen until you are meditating for half an hour a day, perhaps in two 15-minute sessions. Initially, you may need to glance at a clock to remind yourself when to stop. But once accustomed to the practice, you will find yourself moving out of meditation at the appointed time without external help.

Concentration and Breath

Owing to its fundamental importance to meditation, we need now to go more deeply into what is meant by concentration and how it is achieved. By concentration we do not mean the fierce, browbeating intense mental effort that was sometimes demanded of us when mastering lessons at school. In meditation, concentration is far more subtle. The mind rests lightly, but pleasantly and clearly, upon the point of focus. When it strays, it is gently brought back to this point of focus, without irritation or frustration. Negative responses such as irritation and frustration only discourage the mind from reminding us when our attention wanders in the future. After all, why should the mind remind us when all it gets for its pains is our anger? Instead, we should feel gratitude toward the mind for its help. Beginners often say that the mind becomes bored when concentrating on only one thing. Just so – and this is precisely why it wanders off, like a child with a short attention span who is constantly seeking something new.

But as concentration develops, this boredom passes and is replaced by a realization of what can be described as the qualitative experience of life itself. Although we experience what it is to be alive at each waking moment from the day we are born, how often do we pause in order to contemplate what this wonderful experience of life actually is? How often do we stop being distracted by mental chatter and by the world that is outside our heads, and abide instead in the pure experience of just being? Sometimes called *content-less awareness* or *suchness*, this experience of pure being is a taste of the mental state from which all our other mental states arise, a brief glimpse of the very ground of our own nature.

For regular meditation practice, the breath is typically used as the point upon which to remain focused while our chattering minds are busy trying to distract us. Even when using various other techniques mentioned later in the book, it is usual to spend the first few minutes of each session watching the breath, and allowing the mind to become peaceful and still. Use of the breath for this purpose has many advantages. For example, the breath is always with us, so that we can turn to it not only during our meditation sessions but whenever we wish to calm ourselves during the day. In addition, the breath follows a gentle rhythm of inhalation and exhalation which in itself helps to bring a state of peaceful awareness — and if we notice that the breath is shallow or unnecessarily rapid, the very act of deepening it and slowing it down helps to relax and centre ourselves. Above all, concentration upon the breath brings us into direct contact with the moment-by-moment process upon which our very lives depend. The breath has always been linked in the great traditions with the spirit — the invisible, indwelling essence that symbolizes the non-material nature of our true self.

North-South Breathing

Deep breathing promotes health and vitality, and is an excellent stress-reducing technique. It is also a prerequisite to relaxation and meditation. At the beginning of a meditation session, try this yoga technique for balancing and harmonizing the mind and the body. At its simplest, north-south breathing involves blocking off the right nostril with your thumb and inhaling deeply and slowly through the left nostril, then releasing the right nostril and blocking the left one before breathing out. As you do this visualize the air passing through your nostrils as a cleansing light. Repeat the process, but this time breathing in through the right nostril and out through the left. Twelve complete rounds of north-south breathing will sharpen the awareness of the breath.

The breath can be watched either at the nostrils or at the rise and fall of the abdomen, but the former has the advantage in that the sensation at the nostrils is particularly subtle, requiring a more sensitive awareness that helps the development of the meditator's concentration.

If you find it particularly difficult to establish concentration, remind yourself that all meditators have faced and overcome the same difficulty. You can help yourself by counting each breath: initially you can count on both the in-breaths and the out-breaths then, as your concentration improves, count only on the out-breaths. Go from one up to ten, then return to one again — by counting backward if you wish. Should you lose track of your counting, always go back to the beginning and start again. As your concentration develops, extend your counting so that it goes up to 30. If this becomes monotonous, count only on every other out-breath. There is no need to count throughout the whole session. When the mind is suitably quiet you can stop counting for a few breaths, and then go back to it if and when the mind wanders.

When you can focus your attention without counting, dispense with it altogether, but keep it in mind as an effective method for days when your mind is wayward.

When the attention to your breathing is well-established, you will notice additional benefits — that you have become more aware of and in tune with your breathing, and that correct breathing has become second nature. Correct breathing comes from right down in the diaphragm rather than from the upper chest: the contraction of the diaphragm requires minimal energy expenditure and improves ventilation in the lower part of the lungs.

You may also find an increasing affection for your breathing, and for the air flowing into your lungs. There is a sense of harmony with the outer world, of merging with it on each in-breath and out-breath. Some meditators describe a sense of "being breathed" rather than of breathing. Others talk of feeling continuous with the environment, no longer bounded by the surface of the skin. These experiences border upon the mystical, and give life a new and harmonizing dimension.

Focusing the Wayward Mind

Meditation is intended to help us order the confusion of the mind, not to stop us thinking altogether. Most of us discover early on that the mind seems to be largely beyond our control. It has never been trained to know what is expected of it: our education is largely devoted to teaching us facts, and has nothing to do with the mind itself and the potential that lies deep inside it. The gradual training of the mind that occurs with regular meditation enables us to keep focused upon constructive thoughts, to abolish distractions and to progress on our meditative journey.

The mind has many ways of distracting our concentration. It may begin with trivia, but when we refuse to let our mind wander it will go on to more preoccupying matters. It will bring up happy or unpleasant memories, or remind us of pressing things we have to do. Whatever the distraction, just let it go.

see exercise overleaf

Abolishing Distractions

Exercise 9

This exercise represents a tried and tested way of dealing with distractions by categorizing each one as it appears and then mentally "letting it go".

1. Close your eyes and imagine that your mind is the trunk of a tree and all your thoughts are branches. Strong branches with green leaves represent a healthy, focused state of mind, while withered, dying branches are distracting thoughts, feelings and emotions.

2. Now visualize yourself reaching up to the branches of distraction and cutting them from the tree — thus letting go each distraction and freeing your mind to pursue its meditative journey.

3. It is often helpful to categorize each distraction as you cut it down and let it go. Thus you might note "happy memory ... hopes ... anxiety ... unhappy memory ... new idea ... pending task ... regret ... fantasy ...". Once distractions have been categorized in this way, it is as if they recognize that their trickery has been found out, and they withdraw from the scene.

4. Make a promise to yourself that from now on, whenever a distraction enters your mind, you will identify it, and mentally prune your mind's tree of this withered branch.

Prana, Chi and Life Energy

In both Eastern and Western traditions, the breath is associated not only with life itself, but also with the spiritual world and the indwelling spirit in man. The word *inspire* is a good illustration of this: it means both the "in-breath" and an "influx of spiritual or divine influence". (The words *suspire*, *respire* and *expire* all come from the same root, and relate to giving up the breath or spirit.) In the East, the breath has also been linked to *prana*, the Sanskrit word for the non-material life force or energy that is said to be drawn in with the breath. In China this is known as *chi* or *qi*; and in Japan as *ki*.

Chi (which is pronounced "chee") is thought to pass through twelve main channels or meridians in the body. Each channel is associated with a different organ, and along each are points that may be accessed or stimulated to treat physical and

A Meditative Session

Each meditation session has three stages: preparation, practice and conclusion. Awareness of the breath and its life-giving energy form an integral part of each stage. *Preparation* involves gathering the concentration by changing into suitable clothes, carrying out a brief introductory ritual and sitting comfortably on your cushion. To centre your body and increase body awareness, sway from side to side two or three times, then take a few deep slow breaths. *Practice* means the deepening of concentration as your mind turns inward. Allow your awareness to settle at the nostrils where you feel the movement of air as you breathe in and out. *Conclusion* involves a moment of thanks to your mind and body, to your breath and to life itself, and then continued light concentration as you rise from your cushion.

mental disorders caused by blockages to chi. When *chi* flows easily through our bodies, we feel relaxed. But when *chi* becomes blocked by negative thoughts, its flow is hampered, and this may cause stress and ill-health. Current research on the medical efficacy of acupuncture, which uses these channels, tends to support this idea. It is also thought that through the mind power and awareness of the breath developed by the practice of meditation, this life energy can be brought under conscious control, to the benefit both of spiritual development and of physical health (see pp.140–1).

An important first step along the path of meditation is to use the awareness of your breathing to gain insight into the quality of the breaths themselves. The Buddha was very specific about this. In the *Anapana-sati Sutra* (Mindfulness of Breathing) he teaches that:"When breathing in a long breath [the meditator] knows that he breathes in a long breath, when breathing in a short breath he knows that he breathes in a short breath." The meditator thus comes to know whether the breathing is long or shallow; whether it is from the upper chest or from the diaphragm;

whether it flows evenly or is jerky; whether it is fast or slow; whether it is noisy or quiet. The breath reveals a great deal about the meditator's state of mind and his or her state of physical relaxation.

An ancient yoga teaching holds that each person's life span is represented by the number of breaths allocated to them before birth. Quick, shallow breathing uses up the allocation faster than slow, deep breathing, thus shortening life. Like many such teachings, there is an underlying truth to this in that slow, deep breathing is associated with the relaxation of body and mind, which is clearly beneficial both to meditation and to health.

It is important to remember that deep breathing refers not to the length of the breath, but to the fact that breathing takes place from the diaphragm, as low down as possible, rather than from the restricted area of the upper chest. Upper chest breathing is useful after exercise, when the body has an urgent need for oxygen, but during sedentary periods requires unnecessary effort.

The *complete breath*, which some texts advise you to employ two or three times at the start of meditation as an aid to relaxation and concentration, refers to a slow measured breath that commences at the diaphragm, then fills the middle and finally the upper chest until the whole of the lung area is fully expanded. But take care not to hyperventilate (take in too many complete breaths in quick succession), as this can lead to dizziness and even fainting.

The breath can also be used in connection with the power of visualization (see pp.106–7). One simple practice is to imagine the breath flowing into your body in the form of white light and exiting in the form of grey or black smoke that contains all your tensions and tiredness. To do this, allow your awareness to move from its usual place at the base of the nostrils and to extend from the nose down to the abdomen. On the in-breath, the white light is seen as flooding this whole area, absorbing impurities, and then the smoke flows out leaving the body purified. This practice can be combined with north–south breathing (see p.59), and used at the start of each meditation.

The Undistorted View

Central to Buddhist philosophy is the concept of the Middle Way. This incorporates the Noble Eightfold Path, the psycho-spiritual route at the end of which there is enlightenment. The Noble Eightfold Path is divided into three parts. *Right view* and *right thought* lead to wisdom. *Right speech*, *right action* and *right livelihood* belong to the field of ethics. *Right effort, right awareness* and *right concentration* are connected with the practice of meditation.

Right view is also central to all the other great traditions. It refers to the ability to see the world and one's own life without illusion and misunderstanding. Such a view separates the real from the unreal, and is an integral part of the insights that arise in meditation.

Everything changes, nothing remains without change.

The Buddha (568–488BCE)

All things change, nothing perishes.

Ovid (43BCE–18CE)

As you carefully watch the thoughts or the breath in meditation, this view begins to emerge. The first insight is often the realization of the transitory nature of the things that you are watching. The thoughts come, fade away and are then replaced by other thoughts. An in-breath is taken, then replaced by an out-breath, which is then in turn replaced by the next in-breath. As you watch this constant movement, you will suddenly become aware that all things, not just thoughts and in-breaths and out-breaths, are subject to this process of change and renewal. Our happiness and our sadness, the good times and the bad, in fact everything in our world, from the Himalayan mountains to the brief life of the fruit-fly, is governed by the same unalterable law of impermanence. This awareness is very different from an academic knowledge: it is something that is experienced at first hand.

With this experience there often comes a strong commitment to knowing what, if anything, lies behind this ever-changing picture-show of life. We have already uncovered one puzzle, "Who am I?", and now there is another, "What is anything?" And as soon as this second puzzle emerges, it is seen as being closely connected to the first one. In many different ways we and the world around us are inexorably related. Some of these ways are explored in *Exercise 10, Dealing with Illusions* (p.68). Impermanence is clearly one of the most important features of our existence.

If indeed all things in the world of our immediate experience are impermanent, is there something deeper that is eternal? If we look beyond the transience of thoughts, feelings, emotions, in-breath and out-breath, our own body and even the Himalayan

mountains, is there in fact anything to be seen?

As was explained earlier, when the question "Who am I?" was first identified (see p.31), the meditator does not pose the question in order to answer it personally. Rather, the question is left hanging in the air, as if it fills the mind yet does not actually trouble it. If answers come, they will not come through the reasoning and logic of the conscious mind, but from a source that the meditator has not yet had time to recognize. There is no urgency, only a deep and abiding wish to know one's true self, together with the conviction that now the question has been identified, the answer to it will eventually arise.

One way of describing this is to imagine that you are putting the question to a wise and loving friend who sits opposite you, who listens to your every thought, but who knows that the moment is not yet right to give you the answer to your question. Try not to become frustrated by your friend's withholding of the answer: instead, feel comforted by their wisdom, knowledge and desire to guide you.

see exercise overleaf

Dealing with Illusions

One of our biggest illusions is that we are isolated beings, moving through life for ever divorced from other people and from the material world. Meditation progressively helps us to see through this illusion.

1. Begin with the breath. Close your eyes and become aware that you partake of the outer world with each in-breath, and give back with each out-breath. Follow the breath as it enters and leaves the body, and recognize it as the outer world first embracing and energizing the inner world, then serenely carrying away any impurities.

2. Allow your awareness to rest on the outer surfaces of your body, and feel the caress of the atmosphere warming or cooling you, receiving or giving warmth. Be conscious of yourself occupying space, yet being a part of that space. Then allow your awareness to move downward until you feel the solidity of the ground supporting your weight.

3. Listen to the sounds around you. Open your eyes and see the shapes and colours with which the world fills your awareness. Recognize the extent to which the world flows in and through you and you flow in and through it. Feel kinship and gratitude toward the rest of creation.

Resolving Aches and Pains

By observing the minor physical aches and pains that arise during meditation you will learn to recognize that the mind is as easily distracted by bodily discomforts as it is by thoughts (see *Exercise 8, Learning to Sit*, p.55). As with thoughts, many of these discomforts can be seen to be of minor and transitory importance when observed objectively.

Medical research into pain control indicates that this may also be true of chronic physical aches and pains. It would be an over-simplification to say that all pains are in the mind, but it is certainly true that all pains are registered by the mind, and are greatly influenced by the attitude of the mind toward them. To test this, hold an ice cube in your hand for a moment and feel the discomfort this causes. Now tell yourself that you are actually holding a red-hot coal that is searing deeply into the flesh and notice how your discomfort sharply intensifies. This is not to say that we can simply "think" our way out of discomfort, but if we can learn through meditation to control how the mind interprets such aches and pains, so that we can begin to distinguish between real and imaginary pain, we come a step closer to leading healthier, less painful, lives. The human body needs movement for health, but it also needs stillness.

In meditation, immobility of the body helps immobility of the mind. The mind focuses intently on the only thing stirring, the gentle coming and going of the breath. This slight movement within the enclosing stillness becomes the centre of awareness, and any physical discomforts that register upon the mind are viewed from this centre. Instead of being pulled toward them so that they occupy our full attention while the mind dwells on the discomfort they cause (sometimes accompanying this with feelings of irritation, resentment or anger), we view them with a degree of detachment. As meditators are prone to remark, the pain may still be there, but it no longer bothers them. If the mind becomes distracted by the pain, it is brought gently back each time to the breathing. This is not an exhortion to masochism. If you are sitting correctly, discomforts are unlikely to be indications of any real physical distress. In addition, if you have gradually and gently built up the length of your sittings, your body will have had plenty of time to adapt to your meditation posture.

However, the point of your meditation practice is to be comfortable — you are not learning the more rigorous forms of meditation such as a Zen monk might practise. If, after commencing meditation, you experience serious discomforts during or following the session that do not seem to be merely temporary, immediately cut your meditation time to only ten, or even five, minutes each session. Usually the problem will clear up with this reduction in time, but you may want to seek advice from an experienced teacher (see pp.83–5) or medical practitioner.

Our anxieties and unpleasant memories can be dealt with in the same way as physical discomforts. At first, such things tend to surface frequently in meditation. The experience has been likened to the way that bubbles surge to the surface the moment you loosen the top of a bottle of fizzy drink, or to what happens if we abruptly release a tightly wound metal spring. When the restrictive control of the consciousmind is relaxed through meditation, material that is currently absent from the conscious mind (material in the *preconscious*), some of which is unwelcome, rises to the surface. By refusing to do more than observe this material, we find it no longer arouses knee-jerk reactions of anxiety or irritation, and thus it loses its power to dominate awareness. Even recent annoying or embarrassing incidents can be observed calmly and without loss of equanimity. The release of anxieties and unpleasant memories is more likely to be noticed during the first few minutes of meditation, and after that to disappear gradually.

Harmony of the Self

Exercise 11

As we have seen, awareness in meditation is usually of the breathing, but it can be of any part of the body, the thoughts themselves, or external objects. It can embrace the whole body, an exercise that is helpful in enhancing body awareness and encouraging it to operate as a harmonious unit instead of as a collection of disparate and often conflicting parts.

1. Establish concentration by focusing upon the breath, then transfer your awareness to your right arm, from the fingers to the shoulder. Now do the same with your left arm.

2. While remaining aware of your arms, become progressively conscious of your torso and then of your neck, head and face. Your awareness now extends to the whole of your upper body.

3. Without losing this interconnectedness, become progressively aware of each part of the lower body, so that the whole of your physical presence is embraced.

4. Sit in this embrace for the rest of the session. You may experience feelings of gratitude toward your body for the way that it carries out its vital functions without need for conscious control.

Stillness and Silence

The Bible tells us to "be still, and know that I am God". We live in a world that is polluted as much by noise as by toxic waste. Rarely can we listen unhindered to the sounds of the natural world. Our modern way of living separates us from our roots. Over the eons of our existence on this planet we have evolved in constant touch with a silence within which the sounds of wind, water, rainfall and birdsong play from time to time as in a vast theatre. Only in the last 200 years or so have we forsaken natural sounds for the artificial noise of machines that offers no beauty or harmony to the mind and spirit.

The great traditions have always counselled us to retreat back into the natural world from time to time if we are to grow in inner strength and understanding. They even warn us to avoid idle chatter: the more we listen to our own voice and to the voices of others, the more we are aware that so much of our speech is distracting and superfluous. We may notice that many of us talk to cover our awkwardness when in company, or to tell people of our doings and of our preoccupations, even if they show no interest in them. Many of us talk to share (or sometimes to foist) our anxieties, interests and expectations on the rest of the world – and also, of course, to justify, criticize, moan, gossip, complain, boast and protest.

Many of us are afraid of silence, and eager to fill it with sound. When we are not doing the talking ourselves, we are either listening or half-listening to the chatter of the television or radio, or to the beat of pop music. Yet the experience of silence is as necessary to our psychological and physical health as is the experience of open, honest and stimulating communication. In meditation we learn to re-enter this experience. Silence is part of our birthright: meditation allows us to reclaim this birthright, and the inner transformation that it brings. The evidence of this transformation soon becomes apparent in our behaviour. Meditators tend to speak less but to greater effect than in their pre-meditation days. Their interests and activities may move from the frenetic and superficial to the calmer and more contemplative. They may take increased pleasure in works of art, and intuitively share something of the sublime vision of the men and women who created the art. They may take a new delight in nature; face decisions with greater equanimity and insight; see the best rather than the worst in people and in situations; and recapture a sense of awe at the mystery and infinite potential of life.

Paradoxically, experiencing the abiding silence within ourselves lessens rather than strengthens self-preoccupation and an over-concern with our feelings and doings. Sound erects barriers between the self and the rest of the world. Allow-

The quiet and solitary man apprehends the inscrutable. He seeks nothing, holds to the mean and remains free from entanglements.

I Ching (1150BCE)

ing the mind to abide in inner silence helps lower these boundaries, enabling us to recognize that the outer world is not external and separate from ouselves, but something that we experience by actually bringing it within the mind. We register external reality when our senses convey the impressions of it to our brains and it becomes one with the inner world of the conscious mind.

The silence of meditation allows us to carry out a thorough exploration of self. The realization that we are not isolated from the rest of the world grows stronger. Do not worry if this suggests that meditation produces a loss of our usual sense of personal identity — in fact, it opens us to that extended sense of self that reaches out to embrace the whole of creation and experiences the conviction that universal love sustains and unites all things.

see exercise overleaf

In Search of the Self

Exercise 12

You first asked yourself the question "Who am I?" quite early on in this book, and repeated it from time to time throughout your meditation sessions in a light, half-amused way, without expecting an answer – yet. This question remains central to self-discovery, but your practice is now sufficiently well-established for you to supplement it with a variant of an ancient Buddhist exercise that we can call "In Search of the Self".

1. Begin as usual by focusing on the breath, then switch your awareness to a point between and just above the eyes. Ask yourself "Do I live here?"

2. Now move downward to the throat and ask the same question. Then move down to the heart, then to the solar plexus, and to any other part of the body you wish, repeating the same question "Do I live here?" each time.

3. If you find you answer "yes" to any of the questions, ask yourself "Who is it who lives here?" Stay with the question in the same spirit of light, almost playful enquiry you use when asking "Who am I?"

Developing Positive Emotions

Many people believe they are unable to meditate because they cannot "control" their minds. This belief is precisely the root of their difficulty. The purpose of meditation is not to control the mind, but to focus it upon a single point of concentration, so that it no longer identifies with the various distractions that usually capture our attention. By refusing to allow the mind to become lost in its thoughts or identified with unwelcome emotions, meditators find themselves achieving not only inner equanimity, but also the ability to see more deeply into the nature of the self. But meditation can also be used to encourage the development of positive thoughts and emotions. The Tibetan Buddhist "loving kindness" meditation practice is a good example.

By meditation upon light and upon radiance, knowledge of the spirit can be reached and peace can be achieved.

Patanjali (c.300BCE)

In a practice of this kind, the meditator usually starts by building up the sense of gratitude and self-acceptance toward him or herself touched on at the end of *Exercise 11, Harmony of the Self* (p.71). Central to this is the sense of simply being present, as a precious human life, without concerns or longings, without dissatisfactions over life circumstances, and without self-judgments. What is, quite simply is. In letting go of hopes and regrets in this way, the mind settles naturally and effortlessly into self-acceptance, which in many cases then opens into a love

for oneself that is a love for the gift of existence rather than for the limited and limiting personal ego.

Once this positive awareness of self becomes stabilized, the meditator brings to mind someone who feels particularly close, a partner or a son or daughter, or a friend perhaps, and extends the feeling of acceptance and love until it embraces that person. Next the feeling is extended to someone a little less close; then to someone toward whom the feelings are normally neutral; then toward someone who is disliked; then toward someone who arouses actual antipathy. Last of all, the meditation is extended so that the positive feelings are allowed to embrace people in general, and ultimately all sentient beings.

This exercise can be used for situations as well as for people. The meditator first brings to mind a situation in which they feel very much at ease, and allows this relaxed feeling to become fully established. Next comes a situation that evokes rather less positive feelings, followed by one toward which there are neutral reactions, then one which usually raises mild anxiety, and finally one that invokes more disturbing emotions. In each imagined situation, the feeling of being at ease is allowed to become fully established before moving on to the next scenario.

By visualizing positive emotions, meditation helps to reduce anxiety levels, thus making the meditator calmer, less worried and more self-confident. Relaxation and ease of mind are beneficial when any kind of stressful situation is anticipated. For a student who is about to take an examination, or for a prospective employee prior to a job interview, a few minutes of meditation beforehand can help to lessen anxiety and improve one's self-image. Athletes have reported that they use meditation as part of their preparation before competitions, as do some actors before going on stage.

Meditation has also been used successfully in the medical world, to lower the anxiety experienced by patients preparing for a major surgical operation — and even prior to dental treatment.

When using visualization practices, it is important not to move from one person or one situation to another until the requisite positive emotion is fully established. If at first you feel unable to go beyond people close to you or beyond non-stressful situations, stay with these. With practice, it becomes progressively easy to extend our positive emotions further afield.

Meditation, Sleep and Hypnosis

Even if tired to begin with, most meditators find that once the mind becomes focused and relaxed, tiredness quickly evaporates — although if done last thing at night, meditation often prepares the mind for restful sleep. The busy chatter of the mind is responsible for keeping us awake. If you have trouble sleeping, focus upon your breathing when you go to bed, but this time not with the idea of staying alert, as in meditation, but of sinking down into sleep with each breath. Because meditators are able to focus upon a single point of concentration, they often make good hypnotic subjects. They are able to focus upon the voice of the hypnotist and ignore any inner resistance to his or her suggestions. But meditation is not the same as going into a hypnotic trance — few mind states could be less alike.

Working with Others

Meditation is often thought of as a lonely path, with the meditator sitting absorbed in an inner world. However, there have always been two approaches to the context within which one practises: for want of better terms, we might call these "the way of the hermit" and "the way of the monk". In the way of the hermit, the meditator works alone (traditionally withdrawing to a forest, desert or lonely mountain). In the way of the monk, the meditator works with a community of like-minded people (traditionally living in a monastery).

As the majority of meditators are neither hermits nor monks, these terms are used metaphorically. Opportunity and personal preference play a part in deciding which route to take, but there are advantages and disadvantages in both approaches. Working alone avoids reliance on a group, and some people may find that a group meditation turns primarily

into a social get-together. On the other hand, a group can provide support, encouragement and guidance — thus sustaining motivation and helping to avoid problems and wrong turnings. In addition, many people find that the very act of meditating within a group of friendly and compassionate people subtly changes the atmosphere, so that meditation becomes both easier to maintain and a more profound experience.

In general, most meditators value the opportunity of working with a group of like-minded people, so the question arises how can you find such a group. The great majority of groups have an affiliation, formal or informal, with a particular spiritual tradition, or with a particular teacher. This can lead to difficulties if the meditator is expected to adhere to a certain set of beliefs, or follow rituals that he or she finds unacceptable. Also, he or she may find themselves required to pursue a particular meditation practice and to abandon experimentation with any other practice.

Frequent changing from one practice to another is undesirable and likely to hinder progress. In addition, in meditation, as in so many other areas of life, it is wise to be circumspect about any person or organization claiming to have a monopoly of the truth. You should be particularly suspicious about any person or organization more interested in your money than in your progress. You should reject outright any attempts to deprive you of your freedom, or to cajole you to take part in any rituals, practices or relationships, or to enter into any commitments, against your will or even against your better judgment.

If you do find the right group to work with, remember that sitting with a group is not a substitute for your regular daily practice. Groups typically meet once a week or less, and these infrequent sessions will not be enough for your practice to develop. Your aim must be to enjoy the support of the group, but at the same time to have the determination to combine this with your personal daily practice.

Group Meditation in the Workplace

Group meditation has many potential benefits in the workplace. Meditating before beginning the day's work can be an effective way of encouraging creative thought or enhancing productivity – relaxed workers usually handle jobs more efficiently and accurately than tense ones. It has been shown that people who meditate together achieve a greater sense of harmony with those around them; so that before a meeting, for example, the use of group meditation could lead to a greater flow of ideas and more harmonious teamwork. In addition, meditation can improve the health of workers by reducing the frequency of stress-related illnesses. During the working day, short sessions of improvised meditation (see *Exercise 6, Improvised Meditation*, p.45) could help to "recharge the batteries".

Spiritual Awareness

A Hindu meditation text describes meditation as "furnishing the mind with the necessary conditions for ... the manifestation of its highest potential" and also with the deep relaxation without which "the poor overburdened mind seldom gets any rest, even during sleep".

The psychological and physical aspects of this potential have been discussed, but what of the spiritual? It is revealing that both Eastern and Western meditational practices have been developed within the context of the great spiritual traditions.

The spiritual benefits of meditation centre around a deepening awareness of the self as an inner enduring essence, and of our relationship to the source of the numinous forces that create and sustain all life: a source both immanent (within ourselves) and transcendent (above and beyond ourselves). Over the centuries various attempts have been made to describe this source,

The Path to the Truth

Sunyata is a term that is sometimes used in Buddhism for the nature of the path to the truth. Translated as the "void" or "emptiness", *sunyata* is taken by some Western Buddhists to mean annihilation. These people believe that meditation is a way of recognizing that we are nothing more than our physical, perishable bodies, and that death is the end of us. But *sunyata* expresses reality in terms of a dynamic, living universe, and not of a static, dead one. Life itself is movement and change, and the source from which it arises is infinite in its potential to create this continuous movement and change. Meditation asks us to look beyond the physical and impermanent aspects of life and find our true reality in that from which movement and change arise.

but language cannot describe the limitless. Accordingly, much of the world's great spiritual literature eschews description. In Hindu scriptures the source, Brahman (not to be confused with Brahma), is referred to only as "that about which nothing can be said". The Buddha refused to define Nirvana, the final spiritual goal, and Jains refused to define Ishatpragbhara, the ultimate state of the blessed. Even a theistic religion such as Christianity speaks of an ineffable Godhead beyond the revealed God of the Gospels.

As the source of life cannot be described, it can only be known through direct experience – in particular through the experience of meditation. The Buddha stressed that no spiritual teachings should be taken on trust – everything must be tested for oneself. The path to the truth lies through oneself rather than through the second-hand accounts of other people.

see exercise overleaf

Positive Affirmations

Exercise 13

A Hindu meditation that helps us recognize that our true nature lies beyond the physical and apparent is to focus upon three affirmations: "I have a body, but I am not my body; I have thoughts, but I am not my thoughts; I have a mind, but I am not my mind." They can be used separately or together.

1. Begin as usual by focusing on the breath, then switch your awareness to concentrate on the affirmation "I have a body, but I am not my body". Hold the affirmation unswervingly at the centre of awareness. You may find it useful actually to repeat the phrase out loud.

2. Then concentrate on the affirmation "I have thoughts, but I am not my thoughts".

3. Finally, concentrate on the affirmation "I have a mind, but I am not my mind". Try not to become sidetracked at any time by questioning the affirmation's meaning or by your mind's attempts to argue the issue. It is simply a statement, complete in itself. The body is physical, it comes and goes. Thoughts come and go. The mind — feelings, emotions, moods — changes. The meditation impresses upon us we are none of these transitory things.

Teachers and Retreats

You will sometimes hear it said that you cannot make progress in meditation without a teacher. Though it may be true that you are yourself your own best teacher, the value of working with an experienced practitioner is that he or she can not only set you on the right meditative path at the outset, but can also help you deal with any problems and difficulties as they arise. These relate primarily to wandering and distracting thoughts and emotions, and to visions, both pleasant and unpleasant. A teacher can also help to sustain your motivation, and provide support and explanations if, as sometimes happens, feelings of sadness of unknown origin surface during meditation (typically, such feelings are the release of repressed unhappiness accumulated over the years).

When choosing a teacher, use the same care as when choosing a group (see pp.78–9). Look for someone who embodies the qualities that arise from meditation, such as relaxed energy, confidence and a generally well-balanced personality. And remember that a good teacher will win and hold your loyalty through what they have to offer, and not through fear or coercion.

Good meditation teachers are not easy to find, and it is better to work alone, following the guidance of the many comprehensive texts currently available, than to put yourself in the hands of an inadequate teacher. Some meditation teachers will tell you that you cannot learn from books, but these are usually teachers who are over-influenced by Eastern traditions, where books and their power are not always as well-known and appreciated as in the West. It is true that you cannot learn *just* by reading books: you must put into practice what they teach. Books are not a substitute for practice – they are guides to set you on your way. They can motivate, arouse interest and inspire

– and by placing the onus on you rather than on a teacher, they can help you to be more self-reliant and more aware of the personal nature of what you are trying to do.

If you are fortunate enough to find a good teacher, he or she may hold meditation retreats. Alternatively, a number of traditions, including Christianity and Buddhism, operate centres or monasteries where retreats can be taken.

A retreat – which for beginners can be anything from a day to a week – is an opportunity for more intensive meditation practice. Make sure you know in advance what it entails, and do not attempt too much the first time. Retreats usually consist of half-hour stretches of group meditation throughout the day, interspersed with teachings, individual interviews with the teacher to discuss your practice, physical exercises and rest periods. On more demanding retreats the first meditation session may start at 6.30 am, or as early as 4.30 am, and there may be a dozen or more further sessions. A rule of silence may apply even at mealtimes, and rest periods may be devoted to individual meditation. Less demanding retreats will have fewer meditation sessions, and more time for group discussions and private study. Or a retreat may simply be a period of time where, though you are in the company of others, you are left to decide for yourself when and how you want to practise.

The environment of a retreat centre, the silence, the concentration on practice, the presence of the teacher and of other committed individuals, usually mean that more progress is made on a retreat than in many weeks of brief daily sessions (although a retreat is no substitute for these sessions). The first day or two may seem hard, with the mind busier than usual in the novel setting, and physical discomfort more noticeable. You may have doubts about whether you can last the course. But often by the second day the mind experiences a subtle deepening and widening, as if the many boundaries that chop up our inner and our outer worlds are beginning to dissolve into a harmonious flow of simple experience.

Creating a Personal Retreat

Exercise 14

In addition to (or as an alternative to) attending a retreat, some meditators arrange their own private retreats. If this is a possibility for you, choose a day free of commitments and make a few preparations.

1. Draw up a programme for the day. Decide the length and number of your sessions. Four 30-minute sessions may be enough for a start (or six to eight 20-minute sessions).

2. Decide what you are going to do between sessions. If you plan to read, choose texts with a bearing upon meditation. Spend time outside if you have a quiet, private garden. Physical labour is also suitable. Whatever the task, focus mindfully upon it.

3. Prepare food beforehand. Keep meals simple and frugal (for example, bread, fruit and cheese). Avoid elaborate cooking, and drink only water or fruit juice.

4. Have blankets or rugs to hand if it is cold; hunting for them can be distracting.

5. Enlist the co-operation of anyone who lives with you, so that you can keep silent all day.

BEYOND THE GATEWAY

Entering the gateless gate is an auspicious

experience, but it is still only the beginning of the

spiritual journey and beyond the gateway lies a path

without end. The techniques of the great meditative

traditions can help us to progress along this path

into the mysteries of mind and being.

The Great
Traditions

The term "great traditions" refers to those enduring systems of belief, ritual and practice that have profoundly affected civilization and the way in which men and women think about themselves and their lives. Much of the world's greatest music, painting, architecture sculpture, literature and philosophy has been inspired by them.

From earliest times, meditation has featured extensively in these traditions, helping the mind to approach an awareness of its own nature and of the greater reality that expresses itself through the individual mind, whether this reality is experienced as a personal god or as a cosmic force beyond human description and definition. The great traditions share many similarities in their approach to meditation despite their cultural and linguistic differences. The emphasis placed upon the various techniques varies, as does the interpretation of the experiences arising from meditation, but the fact that all the great traditions have discovered and taught meditative practice confirms its great value as a path toward self-understanding and spiritual growth.

B u d d h i s m

Buddhism, of all the great traditions, is the most closely associated with meditation. The Buddha (the "Awakened One") was a real historical figure, born in about 563BCE as Siddhartha Gautama. 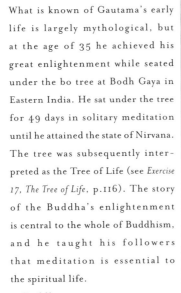 What is known of Gautama's early life is largely mythological, but at the age of 35 he achieved his great enlightenment while seated under the bo tree at Bodh Gaya in Eastern India. He sat under the tree for 49 days in solitary meditation until he attained the state of Nirvana. The tree was subsequently interpreted as the Tree of Life (see *Exercise 17, The Tree of Life*, p.116). The story of the Buddha's enlightenment is central to the whole of Buddhism, and he taught his followers that meditation is essential to the spiritual life.

Buddhism contains many sects, but they can be divided into two main groups: the *Hinayana* and the *Mahayana*. The Hinayana (prevalent in Sri Lanka and South-east Asia) has as its ideal the *arhat*, the person who achieves personal enlightenment and passes into Nirvana, and who recognizes only one Buddha, the historical Buddha (Siddhartha Gautama). The Mahayana (found mainly in Tibet, China and Japan) places more emphasis upon the *bodhisattva*, who vows to return to earth after enlightenment, lifetime after lifetime, in order to teach others, until all can achieve Nirvana. This sect speaks of many Buddhas, some of them Celestial Buddhas (or transcendent energies) who have never been incarnated directly. The term *Hinayana* literally means "the lesser vehicle", and is understandably thought pejorative by southern Buddhists, who prefer the title *Theravadin*, the name of the one surviving Hinayana sect of the many that once flourished.

Although Buddhism does not recognize a creator god, believing that the world has existed from "beginningless time", the Mahayana (meaning the "greater vehicle") has

many gods – beings who either live in the heavenly realms as a result of good karma from earthly lives, or who act as guardians and nature spirits on earth. However, even the gods must one day return to a human life, as only on earth do we find the conditions that inspire and challenge the mind to reach out toward the final enlightenment.

Most Buddhist sects lay particular stress upon the fact that Buddha nature – the enlightened mind – is already within us and can be found through our own effort. However, in the Mahayana it is accepted that bodhisattvas and Celestial Buddhas can help us. The most prominent example of this belief is found in Pure Land Buddhism, which has teachings reminiscent of the relationship between Christians and Christ. Amitabha Buddha, the Celestial Buddha of Boundless Light, is said to rule over a Pure Land (or Western Paradise) which all can enter through devotion to him and by using his mantra (*Namu Amidha Butsu* in its Japanese form) during meditation. The Pure Land is not actually Nirvana itself, but it represents a world where the step to final enlightenment is easier than it is on earth.

Taoism

When Buddhism first arrived in China, it experienced extensive cross-fertilization with Taoism, one of the most important of the existing Chinese religions. Taoism placed particular emphasis upon living in harmony with nature. Any attempts to interfere with the natural order of things, however well-intentioned, were regarded as ill-advised and indeed actively harmful (an insight that the Western world is only now beginning to learn to its cost). The doctrine of *wu wei* (non-interference) taught that everything done by humans should be in keeping with the surroundings; and anything violent or incongruous not only disturbed nature, but also threatened the human spirit. Such a philosophy is based upon a subtle understanding of the inter-relatedness of all things: damage or disrupt even one of these things and the whole pattern is affected (a philosophy that has echoes in modern chaos theory).

In particular, everything has its opposite, the yin and the yang, and the delicate balance between them must be preserved. The essence of this way of thinking is captured in the beauty of traditional Chinese paintings, where nature seems to arrange itself into a haunted stillness that arouses an answering sense of harmony in the human spirit.

Taoist meditation involves the direct contemplation of nature. The mind, unruffled by thoughts, recognizes itself as part of the natural world, not as a superior being with a right to exploit, to change and to desecrate, but as an element within the divine, inseparable mystery of the Tao, which is the all-pervading consciousness.

Taoist meditation also took another, more inward form, which represented nothing short of a quest for immortality. Unlike other religions, which view immortality as a wholly spiritual process, Taoism saw it as arising from a realization

of our full potential, physical as well as mental and spiritual. The actual meditation involved transmuting *ching* (physical energy) into *chi* (mental or subtle energy); *chi* into *shen* (spiritual energy); and then allowing *shen* to become one with Absolute Consciousness itself. It is said that once having achieved this final state, Taoist sages could then practise immortality at any of the levels of being, even living for centuries with unimpaired vitality within their physical bodies.

Taoism is the perfect antidote to the stressful lifestyle of the average Westerner. By allowing the body, mind and spirit to enjoy inner and outer tranquillity, it is possible to create a more harmonious life.

S u f i s m

Sufism is generally regarded as the mystical element within Islam, but some suggest that its roots lie further back in the remote past. Either way, it enjoys a special place within the theistic religions in that it represents an ecstatic longing for, and union with, the Divine that rivals the most intense examples of *bhakti yoga* (see p.118) in the East, coupled with an intensely perceptive understanding of the true nature of the self and its destiny. This combination of heart and head has produced some of our finest religious poetry and inspirational songs.

The form of Sufi meditation best known in the West is the graceful spinning dance of the Mevlevi order (the "Whirling Dervishes"). With the left arm extended palm upward to receive grace from the heavens, and the right arm extended palm downward conveying this grace to the earth, the dancer spins on one heel, turning to the right toward the contemplation of God. With flowing skirts, tall hats and the intense silence in which the movement takes place, the dance has a mesmeric beauty that can initiate the onlooker into a glimpse of the Divine.

The Sufis have another ritual called *dhikr,* which involves constant repetition of the name of God, within both meditation and daily life. Eventually, the name of God spontaneously gives way to the One who is named. This is seen as a gift of grace — God comes to meet those who seek him in love, and draws them out of themselves into a state of divine ecstasy. Self-consciousness disappears, and the Sufi even loses awareness of contemplating God.

Every vestige of separateness disappears, and only God remains, a state that is comparable to the *nirvikalpa samadhi* of the Hindus (see p.92).

Much of the Sufi teaching is done through stories: their oblique wisdom cloaks essential truths that are difficult to convey in less enigmatic ways. Often the first reaction of the listener is to reject the story, but this is followed by a desire to know what lies behind the apparent nonsense. This "desire to know" leads into the silence of meditation, holding the story in the forefront of the mind until it prompts insights into underlying truths.

Sufi Stories

Sufis consider that the ordinary transmission of knowledge is subject to so much editing and false memory that it is no substitute for the direct perception of fact. Teaching stories are a way of facilitating this direct perception. Two of the bestknown stories are both concerned with light. In the first, a man is searching for a lost key in the street. A passer-by stops and offers to help. "Where exactly did you lose the key?" "In my house." "Then why search in the street?" "There is more light out here." In the second, a man is looking for a lamp shop. He stops for directions and is asked, "But why do you want to find a lamp shop?" "I have heard they supply devices that allow you to read in the dark." "That is correct, but there is a prerequisite." "What is that?" "You must already be able to read."

Hinduism

In the Western world Hinduism is often thought of as a single religious tradition, but in fact it is a vast system that covers an incredibly diverse range of beliefs and practices, and one that recognizes no distinction between religion, psychology and philosophy. It probably originated in a variety of faiths ranging from the worship of nature spirits to the worship of Brahman, the source and moving essence of the universe. Even in modern Hinduism, many rural communities still revere local gods whose powers extend only to the borders of their village. Once outside the village, devotion is transferred to universal deities, such as Vishnu and Shiva.

Because of its panoply of gods and goddesses, Hinduism is often thought of as pantheistic. However, at its deepest and most consistent philosophical level, all divine manifestations are seen as aspects of Brahman, about whom nothing can truthfully be said as "he" lies beyond human understanding (although the term *sat chit ananda* (meaning "being, consciousness and bliss") is often used). Within material existence, Brahman is said to manifest as the trinity that comprises Brahma, who is the creator of the visible universe; Vishnu, who is the preserver of this creation; and Shiva, who is the agent of change and movement. Shiva is often depicted with matted hair, symbolic of his asceticism, with a stream of water flowing from his head. He is in deep meditation, either on Mount Kailasa, his mythical Himalayan retreat, or in a cremation ground, where he sits naked, covered with ashes and garlanded with snakes. From his intense meditation, which can last for thousands of years, comes Shiva's great wisdom, symbolized by his third eye.

Each of the three gods has a female consort who appears in various forms, and who gives birth to his energies. Brahma, whose work is completed, is rarely worshipped, and it is Vishnu and Shiva, together with

their consorts (Lakshmi as goddess of wealth and Parvati as the divine mother), who are the main objects of devotion. Various incarnations of Vishnu, such as Rama and Krishna, also have devotees.

Hindus believe that the visible world is *maya*, an illusion that is created by our inability to see the true nature of reality (a belief that resonates in some ways with the modern scientific view that matter is really composed of a subatomic flux of energy). Similarly, our concept of ourselves is also thought of as *maya*, an illusion that can be dispelled only by practices such as meditation that allow us to see through the limited, conditioned self, and recognize that our true nature is the *atman*, the indwelling spirit or soul, which is actually one with Brahman.

Hindu Meditations

In most branches of Hinduism, a particular emphasis is placed on devotion (*bhakti*). The devotee turns the mind always to the divine, and when the deepest level of meditation (*samadhi*) is reached, the meditator may either experience unity with Brahman (*nirviikalpa samadhi*), or enjoy contemplation of one of "his" divine manifestations (*saviikalpa samadhi*). In addition to turning the mind toward the divine, the devout Hindu practises the *sandyhas* (the twilight meditations) which are performed at dawn and dusk, and sometimes at noon, when the sun is at its height. After bathing, washing the mouth and sipping water, the meditator carries out breathing exercises to cleanse the body and mind, then stands and recites an extract from the *Rigveda*, one of the oldest scriptures, dating from around 1200BCE. Water is then scooped up and poured out from the joined palms as an offering to the sun (the symbol of the divine), while the meditator focuses upon the divine itself.

A member of the family carries out the five great sacrifices (*pancamahayajna*s) every day, offering food and meditations to the five kinds of beings – Brahman himself, the ancestors, the gods, the spirits and human beings.

Sometimes animal symbolism is used to represent the particular energies of a god. Thus Ganesh, the elephant god, represents the power to overcome all obstacles on the

Let us meditate upon that excellent glory of the divine vivifying Sun;

May he enlighten

Our understanding.

Rigveda (c.1200BCE)

path of wisdom, while Hanuman, the monkey god, symbolizes self-less devotion and spiritual ingenuity. Vishnu is sometimes symbolized by the fish, and Shiva by the energy of the cobra. The cow, sacred to all Hindus, symbolizes the divine energies that gestate and nurture all living creatures. Each of these symbols can be used as a focus in meditation, allowing the meditator to penetrate deeper into the levels of consciousness where, for each level, corresponding spiritual energies reside.

Om is one of the most sacred symbols within the Hindu tradition. By reciting this mystic syllable, a person is thought to gain access to the powers of the universe, and meditation on *Om* is said to lead to enlightenment and immortality. (See *Exercise 20, Using a Mantra*, p.125.)

Westerners often question why certain Hindu sects practise extreme austerities, take vows of silence or adopt uncomfortable postures — for example, remaining standing or holding arms aloft, for months or even years on end. The answer to that question is that such practices provide a constant reminder of the need to focus on the divine, and help to subdue the bodily cravings that hinder spiritual realization.

Jainism

The ideal of *ahimsa*, non-violence, is an essential feature of both Hinduism and Buddhism, but is carried to its furthest extreme in Jainism. Jains avoid any activity that involves taking life, even refraining from tilling the soil or eating root vegetables in case they harm tiny insects. Jain monks traditionally wear breathing masks to prevent inhaling small insects, and brush the ground ahead of them as they walk. Monks of the Digambara sect forswear clothes, both to avoid harming insects that settle on the body and to demonstrate poverty and renunciation. Thus Jain *tirthankaras*, or saints, are often depicted meditating nude, with their arms held a few inches away from their bodies (the *kayotsarga* posture), a position that symbolizes penance, harmlessness and the supremacy of the mind over the body.

The Western Traditions

We have discussed the place of meditation in the Christian Orthodox Churches of Greece and Russia (see p.20), but meditation has also played an important part in other areas of Western life, in particular in the so-called "mystery traditions". Originating in Egypt and the Middle East, these traditions reached their peak around the sixth and fifth centuries BCE in the philosophical schools of ancient Greece, and their influence has lived on in the so-called occult fraternities that still exist today.

One of the most distinguished of these schools was that of Pythagoras, who is better known today as a mathematician. Pythagoras himself studied the mysteries of Egypt, Chaldea, Babylon and probably those of the Hindu gods. The Greeks, students of philosophy (meaning "love of wisdom"), sought answers to fundamental questions through direct experience of higher levels of being and not merely through reason. Students at Pythagoras's school spent the first five years of study in silence, meditating and following a course of instruction that they did not question. Subsequently, if suitable, they were initiated into the mysteries. The details of the mysteries have never been revealed, but they appear to have involved out-of-body experiences (see pp.148–9) during which the meditator entered the next world and the spiritual realms.

Contemplation is a variant of meditation much used in the West, particularly in the Christian tradition. For example, the meditator attains a state of devotional rapture by gazing at a holy symbol or image. A non-Christian form of this meditation focuses upon the pictures of the Tarot Major Arcana (see illustrations opposite), allowing each in turn to take the mind on a symbolic journey toward an ultimate goal of self-realization. Scrying is another form of contemplation that was much used in the Western tradi-

HOUSE OF GOD

THE STAR

tion. The meditator gazed at a shiny surface or into a glass or crystal ball, while keeping the mind empty of thoughts. Clairvoyant images sometimes appeared, or the meditator experienced periods of disassociation in which he or she appeared to pass through into another world.

A technique that was used in some Western magical traditions involved two meditators taking an inner journey together. Somewhat akin to co-hypnosis, the meditators built up an elaborate visualization of a scene — such as a Greek temple or an enchanted forest — each of them contributing details in turn.

The technique involved a great deal of practice, because each detail had to be fully stabilized in the minds of both meditators before proceeding to the next. When the visualization was properly established, the meditators visualized themselves entering the scene and continuing their meditation in the world of their shared imagination.

It was said that if two meditators were closely attuned to each other, the whole exercise could be done silently in direct mind-to-mind communication, a development that claimed to allow the meditators to enter higher worlds together.

Vision and Sound

When focusing upon the breath in meditation we are using our sense of touch (the subtle sensation of the breath entering and leaving the nose). It is equally possible to use one of the other senses as a focal point. If we burn incense, our awareness can be allowed to rest upon the scent with each in-breath, and upon its absence with each out-breath. This is a highly rewarding meditation, but difficult to sustain for any length of time.

For some purposes, vision or sound are the more appropriate senses to use. When using vision for your basic practice, begin as usual by focusing on the breath, then change to focusing on a picture, geometrical pattern or shape – observed directly or held in the mind as a visualization.

Sound can also be used to great effect in meditation. Chanting, plainsong and sacred music all put us into an altered state of consciousness in which we can experience being taken out of ourselves. One way of using sound is to employ a mantra – *Om Mani Padme Hum* is one of the most widely used mantras in the Tibetan Buddhist tradition.

Although it is not advisable to keep changing one's focus of concentration, it is valuable to experiment with the senses.

The Power of Imagination

As children, we are often taught that imagination is to be dismissed. Many of us can recall an adult saying to us "It's *only* your imagination". But, rather than being the perpetrator of wayward thoughts, imagination not only prompts great works of art and discoveries in science, it also has the power to influence the mind and body. Sports psychology suggests that if you imagine yourself as a successful sportsperson, this can improve your overall performance. Psychotherapy shows that the same is true in personal development, and health psychology indicates that imagination can help the body's powers of self-healing.

For many centuries, in both Eastern and Western thought, no hard line was drawn between the images and sounds conjured up by the mind and those originating in the outside world. The undeniable truth was recognized that wherever images come from, they are *experienced* within one and the same mind. This truth still forms part of the way of thinking of the great meditative traditions. Moreover, it is acknowledged within these traditions that the strength of our imagination depends in large measure upon frequency and quality of use. The downgrading of the importance of imagination to which we are often subjected in childhood, the overemphasis upon materialism, and the relative neglect of the arts, rob us of much of our power to make use of our imaginative talents.

These talents can be rediscovered through meditation. This does not mean that we start to hallucinate or to confuse the inner and outer worlds, simply that we become able to use the imagination to enrich the colour and texture of life, and to enhance our ability to realize our full potential.

Visualization (see pp.106–7) is the form in which the imagination is

most often used in meditation, but we can also imagine the experience of our other senses – such things as *hearing* a favourite piece of music, or *smelling* the scent of a flower, or *stroking* a cat. Initially, these imaginings may be fleeting and tenuous, but practice helps them to become more vivid.

In the same way, we can imagine feelings and emotions. The *loving kindness* meditation (see p.76) is one example of this, in that the more we can *imagine* feelings of compassion and friendship toward casual acquaintances, and maybe even toward people whom we dislike, the more successful the actual experience is likely to be. We can also imagine happiness for ourselves, or sympathy or empathy for others. Any feeling that is evoked by direct experience is capable of being evoked by the imagination, and once imagined, the more readily the feeling arises in daily life.

When you are imagining feelings and emotions, first allow awareness of the breathing to move from the nose to the solar plexus – the second largest concentration of nerves in the body – and *imagine* how this area feels in happiness (or sadness, or whatever). Sometimes the results are surprisingly rapid; sometimes they take longer. However, you will find that perseverance always pays.

Visualization

Visual imagination is used in many different ways by the great meditative traditions, but central to them all is the process of personal development. In Buddhism the practitioner visualizes the Buddha, then imagines him coming to rest within the heart's energy centre, or *chakra*, thus taking into oneself (or arousing from one's own potential) the Buddha's transcendent qualities. In Christianity, some of the best examples of visualization are in St Ignatius Loyola's *Spiritual Exercises* (c.1540), which form part of the training of the Jesuits. Here, the meditator is given instructions on the visualization of a number of scenes from Christ's life, and then told to place himself within the scene as a servant or a worshipper, absorbing divine grace.

In all work of this kind, the success of the meditation depends largely upon the detail with which the visualization is built up. The

---

Spiritual Shapes

In the Western mystery traditions, geometrical shapes, such as triangles and circles, were extensively used in the training and practice of visualization. Such shapes are not only relatively easy to hold in the mind's eye, they also carry profound symbolic meaning. For example, the upward-pointing triangle represents the aspiration of the human spirit toward God; while the downward-pointing triangle represents the descent of the Divine Spirit into matter. The circle represents the absolute, which is without beginning or end. The meditator focuses upon the chosen image for as long as possible without blinking, then closes his or her eyes and visualizes the image being drawn into the space in between and just above the eyes, the so-called "third eye".

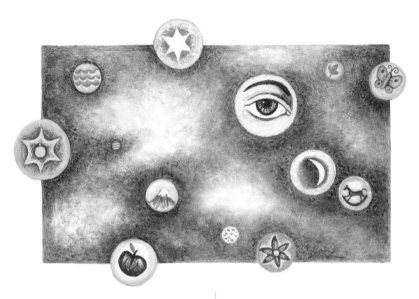

ability to see the detail comes with practice, and there are a number of exercises that can assist the process. One of the simplest is to look at the scene in front of you, then close your eyes and try to retain the image of what you have just seen. At first, results may be disappointing, but soon, as you learn to hone your powers of concentration, the image will seem to float in the space between and above the eyes.

Alternatively, you may like to visualize a favourite journey. Try not to hurry: see each turn of the road, each building, each street name. If you are preparing for a stressful examination or interview, visualize the scene in similar detail, then put yourself within it, retaining the relaxed state of mind. Positive visualization in this way helps to combat the negative self-image that prevents us from realizing our full potential. When using these visualization exercises, decide what you are going to do before you begin, and stick to it. You should not change direction during the session: this weakens self-discipline and encourages intrusive thoughts. Always start by watching the breath, and then move to the visualization once body and mind are settled.

The Palace of the Gods

Mandalas and yantras are the most elaborate symbolic pictures used in meditative visualization. A major part of most Eastern traditions, mandalas and yantras take the meditator on a wordless journey into the deep mysteries of the mind.

Mandalas symbolize cosmic forces in the form of divine beings or Celestial Buddhas. These beings are often surrounded by lesser divinities who represent separate aspects of their powers, and are placed within geometrical shapes that represent their distinctive realms or Buddha fields (areas of activity). When we meditate with a mandala we should focus upon the divine beings either as transcendent spiritual influences or as aspects of our own inner potential. As the power of the practice increases, we may be able to merge our consciousness with the mandala, actualizing within ourselves the qualities it represents.

Yantras differ in that they avoid the use of human or animal forms, and rely upon the symbolism of the geometrical shapes themselves. The best-known yantra is the Hindu *Shri-Yantra* (Yantra of the Illustrious One; see *Exercise 15, Using a Yantra* p.110), of which there are many examples. It consists essentially of nine superimposed triangles converging on a central point (the *bindu*). The *Shri-Yantra* symbolizes the universe in its uncreated, unmanifest form. It provides a graphic representation of the cosmic field of creation, with the triangles representing the union of Shiva and Shakti, the divine forces of male and female, passive and active, potential and realization, which bring the levels of the world of form into being.

When meditating on the *Shri-Yantra*, advanced practitioners allow their minds to reverse the process of creation and travel back through each level of the world of form until they discover in the *bindu* their own formless origins, and then become one with it in the experience of *sarva-anandamaya* (absolute bliss). Thus both mandalas and yantras serve the same essential purpose of taking the meditator to the source of all things. Carl Jung, one of the most influential Western psychotherapists, noticed that as his clients made progress on the healing journey, mandala-like shapes began to appear spontaneously in their drawings and paintings. In his view such shapes originate from within the collective unconscious, and are universal symbols of the wholeness of the authentic self. Certainly mandalas and yantras, in various forms, have occured in all cultures. For example, the maze, a form of yantra consisting of geometrical shapes leading to a central goal, appears in pagan and in Christian art.

Ideally, to make full use of the transforming powers of the mandala or yantra, we should be initiated into the subtleties of their symbolism. But even without the esoteric knowledge needed to penetrate their subtlety, they help concentration in meditation and bring about a deep inner transformation. Their images speak directly to the unconscious, producing an experience of profound harmony and a mystical sense of oneness with the spiritual forces that they represent.

see exercise overleaf

Using a Yantra

Exercise 15

The *Shri-Yantra* (pictured above) is an appropriate visualization tool for both beginners and advanced practitioners, but you can use any mandala or yantra that appeals to you.

1. Place the image at eye level, a comfortable distance from your meditation seat. Use soft but adequate lighting.

2. Sit comfortably on your cushion and close your eyes.

3. To help concentration, watch the breath as usual, and when body and mind become still, open your eyes and focus on the image.

4. Blink only when necessary. Your eyes may have a tendency to flit from one part of the image to another. Try to keep them as still as possible.

5. Ignore any thoughts you may have about the image. Do not attempt consciously to decode its symbols. Allow the symbols to work upon the unconscious. Sense that the image is both in front of you and inside your mind.

The Martial Arts

The martial arts consist of various Eastern philosophies of both self-defence and single combat techniques, such as akido, kendo, tai chi and karate. As they are linked with conflict, it may seem surprising that they are also associated with the peaceful world of the meditator. In fact, success in the martial arts depends to a large extent upon proficiency in meditation. The two are linked at a number of points by a common philosophy.

In their pure form, the martial arts demand the intense awareness of the meditative mind, and have nothing to do with anger or wanton aggression. A practitioner is taught from the outset that the skills must never be used for personal gain, but only in self-defence or in the protection of others – and even then only enough force as is absolutely necessary should be used. The aim must be to disarm and restrain the opponent rather than to inflict injury. (Popular films depicting the martial arts as very violent often give quite the wrong impression.) Furthermore, having to resort to the martial arts in the first place is considered to be a form of defeat, indicating that the individual lacked sufficient inner strength and equanimity to resolve the situation by a more peaceful means.

Central to the martial arts in this pure form is the conviction that the outer expresses the inner. Thus if the mind is in the right place, the outer behaviour, in daily life as well as when practising the martial arts, will always be impeccable. If the mind is in the wrong place, martial arts may be practised for many hours a day for a lifetime, and yet the practitioner will never manifest the spontaneity and purity of action upon which success depends.

Having the mind "in the right place" means having a mind that is so completely focused upon what is happening in the present moment that any action undertaken by an opponent is registered in the instant before he or she actually moves, so that a response can be made even before he or she strikes. The action of the practitioner is thus instantaneous, without the intrusion or mediation of thought. Action of this kind does not arise from a form of so-called muscular memory that responds without the need for prior processing by the central nervous system, as in the reflex action of the tennis player or the boxer. In the martial arts instantaneous action is thought to stem from a form of spiritual energy that is constantly available when you are acting in harmony with the natural world.

In his classic text *Zen in the Art of Archery* (which was written in 1953 but has been continuously in print, and is regarded as one of the few really authentic books on Zen written by a Westerner), the German philosopher Eugene Herrigel tells of his six-year struggle while living in Japan to realize this spiritual energy through the study of archery. His task was deceptively simple — to release the arrow from the high tension of the bowstring without a jerk of the hand. Only then, he was told, would the arrow fly straight and true to the intended target. Yet try as he might, there was always the tell-tale jerk each time the arrow left the bow, and each time the arrow missed the target. Herrigel's teacher, Zen Master Kenzo Awa, sees at once the source of his difficulty. "You have a too willful will" he explains. "You think because you do not do it, it will not happen ... Let 'it' happen through you."

"It" is what I have called "spiritual energy". Herrigel's "wilful will" is the desire of the Western mind to be the conscious doer of its actions, and it is this desire that prevents Herrigel from, as Kenzo Awa puts it, "standing egoless at the point of highest tension". Finally, "it" happens, and Herrigel succeeds in releasing the arrow smoothly and effortlessly. Turning to the Master he confesses wonderingly, "I do not know whether it is I who shoot or whether 'it' shoots me." The Master nods in recognition and then says quietly, "the bowstring has cut right through you." The archer has shot the arrow without ego, and thus the archer, the arrow and the target have become one.

Kinhin

Exercise 16

Meditation is a continuous pathway. Even in the early stages we are on the same journey as those further along the road. As in the martial arts, the *kinhin*, or walking meditation, teaches us the oneness between inner awareness and outer movement.

1. Choose a space that allows you to walk straight ahead for at least a dozen short paces. Make a fist with your left hand. Keep it turned so that your thumb faces inward. Exerting gentle pressure with your right hand, press your left hand against your abdomen just below the navel. Look at the ground ahead.

2. Now lift one foot, with total awareness of each movement in the ankle and leg, and the feeling in the sole of the foot. Take a very short pace forward and put your foot on the ground, feeling the new sensations under the sole.

3. Take further paces with the same awareness. Go as far as you can, then retrace your steps. Keep your movements slow and deliberate, yet smooth and flowing throughout and focus your mind intently on your legs and feet.

The Kabbalah

Kabbalah is the mystical aspect of Judaism, expressing the archetypal structure of the cosmos, of society, and of the individual psyche. It is concerned with the timeless problem of learning the purpose of human life, and of showing how life relates to the universe and God.

The Hebrew word *Kabbalah* means "what is received". Some people interpret this as meaning a tradition, passed down from one generation to another. Others perceive it as knowledge that has been handed down directly from Heaven.

The Kabbalah's precise origins are disputed. Some occult traditions place them in Egypt, attributing authorship to the legendary Hermes Trismegistus; other traditions place them in Greece, with the equally legendary Cadmus as the author. However, Jewish mysticism teaches that the Kabbalah originated in an oral tradition dating back to Adam and was amplified by the divine revelations entrusted to Abraham and to Moses. From the 9th century onward Jewish Kabbalists based in Spain reified the Kabbalah into one of the most coherent and widely used mystical system available in the West.

The Kabbalah is still alive and continuing to provide meaning, growth and spiritual renewal to all those who study it, despite being so ancient in origin. The vast body of knowledge accumulated over centuries has undergone many changes, adapting to different places and periods. However,

It is like a ladder in the midst of his home whereby he may ascend and descend.

Hekalot text
(6th century CE)

the complexities of the Kabbalah are such that traditionally no one should commence the study of this hidden aspect of the Torah until they have reached the age of at least forty and have an experienced teacher and considerable previous acquaintance with spiritual and mystical practice.

Nevertheless, one aspect of the Kabbalah is reasonably accessible, in its simplified form, to the serious meditator. For those with good powers of visualization, the Tree of Life can provide extraordinary insights into progressively deeper and deeper levels of the creative mind (or into higher and higher levels of spiritual realms, if you prefer to think of it in this way). In essence, the Tree of Life is a map of the various levels through which the transcendent power of God descends into, and manifests, the material world. As with the *Shri-Yantra* (see p.110), the meditator reverses the path of these emanations and ascends upward through the levels.

The Tree of Life reflects the belief (that is also found in Eastern traditions) that equilibrium is the universal law of the material world, and that God, the First Cause, manifested two balancing and interdependent forces at the moment of creation. In the Tree of Life we see these two forces emanating from *Kether* (the Crown), and descending along two parallel, opposing but complementary paths until they create and interpenetrate the physical universe (*Malkuth*), which itself then serves as the complementary principle, the mirror-image, of Kether. As they descend, these dual forces manifest the *sefirot*, the intermediate creative, guiding principles. Within the parallel paths, generated from the pure equilibrium between them, are other *sefirah* that express the presence of spirit in matter.

Everything that happens in the physical universe is said to be explicable in terms of the complementary sefirah on the Tree of Life, with disaster arising when humans interfere with the natural order of things and disrupt the balance between them. When the balance is maintained, the Kabbalah promises to humankind the absence of sin and sickness, abundant provision of everything needful, communion with God and the angels, the gift of languages and prophecy, and the power to transmute metals and to work miracles.

see exercise overleaf

The Tree of Life

Exercise 17

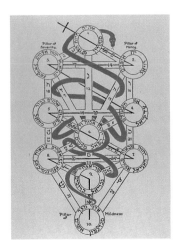

A simplified form of meditation upon the Tree of Life is to hold the concepts represented by each of the *sefirot* as the focus of concentration in a series of meditation sessions.

1. Watch the breath and focus on the concept of the natural, visible world (Malkuth). *Try not to let your mind set off on a train of associations, or extended definitions.*

2. From there, move on to the concept of human consciousness (Yesod); *victory of the higher self over one's basic instincts* (Netzah); *an awareness of the glory of the Divine* (Hod), *the beauty as one realizes the Divine within oneself* (Tifereth); *the Divine mercy and love* (Hesed); *the Divine power* (Gevurah); *the Divine wisdom* (Hokmah); *the Divine understanding* (Binah); *and finally the Divine essence or crown* (Kether). *Beyond Kether lies* Ain Soph, *the formless absolute, analogous to Brahman and the Godhead.*

3. As you meditate on each of the sefirot, you will sense its potential within yourself, each sefirot thus representing the Divine immanence as well as the Divine transcendence.

The Five Yogas

The practice of yoga (a Sanskrit word meaning "yoke", symbolizing union with the Divine) is inextricably linked to the use of meditation in its various different forms. Of the many paths within yoga, the five that are the most widely followed are *hatha yoga, karma yoga, gnana yoga, bhakti yoga* and *raja yoga*.

Hatha yoga, the best-known path in the West, is the yoga of the physical body. Superficially, the intricate postures (or *asanas*) of which it consists help to keep the body supple. At a deeper level, they are said to exert subtle pressure upon the glands and internal organs in the interests of optimum health. At the deepest level of all, they are said to enable the yogi (a yogic devotee) to gain control over the body's vital energy and transmute it into spiritual enlightenment.

Karma yoga, which is the yoga of good works, emphasizes service to others, thus transforming self-cherishing energies into the compassionate love for others that is an expression of the Divine.

Gnana yoga, the yoga of intuitive wisdom, involves the single-minded examination of the mind and of human existence until the true nature of all things is revealed and the yogi becomes one with the Divine vision.

Bhakti yoga, the yoga of devotion, consists of ceaseless outpourings of love toward the Divine, so that the separate self becomes one with the object of this love.

Raja yoga, the yoga of the higher self, focuses upon training the mind until it obtains direct experience of its relationship with the Divine.

Realizing the Divine is thus a major concern of all five types of yoga. At its simplest, we could say that hatha yogis use meditation to focus awareness upon the energy systems within material existence; karma yogis use it to arouse loving compassion toward all sentient beings; gnana yogis employ it to turn the attention toward the intuitive understanding at the deeper levels of consciousness; bhakti yogis use it to dwell on the name and attributes of God; and raja yogis direct it toward that mental purification that raises one toward the ineffable experience of the Divine.

In practice, although most yogis focus chiefly on one of the yogas, elements of them all can be called upon. In fact, all five arise from the practice of any one of them. For example, gnana and raja yoga help develop the compassion associated with karma yoga, the devotion to the Divine associated with bhakti yoga, and the elevation of physical energies associated with hatha yoga. Similarly, the transmutation of physical into spiritual energy yielded by hatha yoga enables the wisdom and mind control of gnana and raja yoga to develop, and inspires the love that is associated with bhakti yoga. (Contemporary Eastern sages teach that bhakti yoga is the most suitable yoga for the degenerate age in which we are said to live.)

Only Eastern traditions use the term yoga, but all meditative and devotional practices can be listed under one or other of the five yogic paths. By the same token, each of the great traditions, although including all five types of yoga, lays emphasis upon a particular path. The shamanic customs stress the importance of recognizing divinity in the physical world (hatha yoga); the theistic religions stress the importance of devotion to God (bhakti yoga); the non-theistic religions emphasize self-exploration (gnana yoga); the mystical traditions seek for union with the inexpressible (raja yoga). All the major traditions emphasize the importance of good works (karma yoga).

Another way of approaching the five yogas is through the teachings of Hindu sages that the Divine can variously be thought of as possessing both form and attributes (as in the natural world); as without form but possessing attributes (as in abstract qualities such as absolute love or goodness); and finally as without form or attributes (as in the numinous, which can be only directly experienced).

Letting Go

Exercise 18

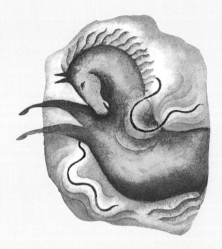

Central to all five yogas is the concept of "letting go". Letting go of the small individual self who stands opposed to the natural world, to other people and to the Divine. All meditation practices can help with letting go, but it is useful to incorporate the following into your meditation programme. Letting go is easier if you identify what you want to release.

1. Start by tensing each of your main muscles, then letting them go. Experience the deep relaxation that follows.

2. Now transfer your attention to the mind. Think about the past, then remind yourself that life is an inexorable process of letting go of each passing moment. Once gone, each moment is as irrecoverable as the birth of the universe itself. Be aware with each breath of letting go.

3. Next, think of your own life. Did you bring it into existence? Do you keep it in being? Do you determine its destiny? Does it in any real sense belong to you? Let go of the sense of "owning" your life. Be aware only of it flowing through you. Let go of any sense of separation between yourself and the rest of life, or of separation between yourself and the source of life.

The Four Elements

Modern science uses the term "elements" for substances that cannot be split chemically into simpler substances. The ancients, however, understood the term to mean something quite different: they spoke only of "four elements" — earth, air, fire and water (plus a fifth, metal, in Chinese culture). These were the four forms in which the visible world presented itself to them. *Earth* represented apparent solidity, from the highest mountain to the smallest plant. *Water* represented liquid in all its forms; *fire*, warmth; and *air*, the breath and anything intangible (including the soul).

Each of the four elements could be used as a focus for meditation, and particular reverence was paid to the point at which one element was transformed into another — for example, the point at which water was seen to move into earth when it fell as rain. Smoke was held to be especially sacred because it arose from the combination of earth (in the form of wood) fire and air — as was water when it was thrown on the flames to produce steam. The human body also combined the four elements — the solidity of bone and flesh, the air in the lungs, the liquid of blood and saliva, and the warmth of the whole body — and was recognized as arising from the same source as the rest of the world, and therefore as one with it.

Great emphasis was placed upon the elements by the shaman, who has been a key figure in human society since earliest times. Shamanism is a set of similar beliefs rather than a unified religion, and it is centred upon a deep awareness of, and reverence for, the life forces of the natural world. It was particularly associated with Siberia, Africa, North America and Tibet, and with the Inuit and the Celts.

Originating primarily in hunter-gatherer societies, shamanism had little conception of tribal or personal "ownership". All land belonged to the great spirits, and was revered and cherished as sacred, while even the mountains and rivers were held to be conscious. Animals were believed to represent spiritual forces and to confer power upon humans by imparting nature's secrets, by providing food, clothing and shelter, and also by acting as guides to other worlds. The shaman (the priest or medicine man) was able to journey to these other worlds, and typically went through an initiation of being torn to pieces by the spirits and then made whole again and reborn into a higher level of awareness. Afterward, the shaman could understand the language of the animals, converse with the spirits of the dead, divine the future and heal the sick.

A range of meditation techniques were practised so that the shaman could attain the state of consciousness that was needed if the soul was to leave the body and go on its other-world journeys. Many of these techniques involved fasting, long periods of solitude, extreme mortification of the body, and focusing the attention upon the sounds of rhythmic drumming.

see exercise overleaf

Finding the Elements

Exercise 19

By meditating in turn on each of the four elements within ourselves, we can emphasize its oneness with the human body. Spend plenty of time per element — one meditation session for each if you wish.

1. Make yourself comfortable in your usual meditation posture and begin with **earth***. Focus upon the solidity of your body as you sit, and feel yourself becoming heavy.*

*2. Then, move to the feeling of warmth (***fire***) pervading every part of your body, beginning at your toes and sweeping upward.*

*3. Next, focus on the sense of the blood (***water***) flowing through each vein and artery. Now, breathe deeply and feel the expansion of the abdomen and chest as* **air** *fills the lungs.*

4. Return to focusing on your body. Extend your awareness so that it feels unity with the earth. As your feeling of heaviness returns, imagine that your body and the earth are one. Now feel one with the warmth, moisture and air outside you. Try not to question whether the feelings of unity between the elements within your body and those outside are objective or imaginary.

Mantras

Eastern traditions teach that all things are composed of vibrating energies. These vibrations are akin to sounds, and the universe itself is thought to have been created by the primal sound *Om*. (In the Christian tradition St John's Gospel also tells us that in the beginning was the *Word*.)

By using certain sounds, the person chanting is thought to be able to influence the vibrations in his or her own body, and thereby his or her physical health and spiritual development. Chanting therefore occupies an important role in the rituals and meditations of all the great traditions. Examples include plainsong (unaccompanied music sung in unison by Christian monks with the aim of producing power-ful changes of consciousness) and the soaring beauty of the oratorios and requiems in sacred music, which aim to lift the soul toward God. The chanting of Buddhist monks, and the low groan of Tibetan horns, provide further examples, as does the Islamic call to prayer, and the intonements of the Jewish religion.

Some languages are thought to be richer in vibrations and harmonies of sacred sound than others. This is particularly true of Sanskrit, which in the East is said to be the primal language, and also of Arabic and Hebrew. It is claimed that to translate these languages is to lose much of their power, because although words can be translated, their vibrational forces cannot.

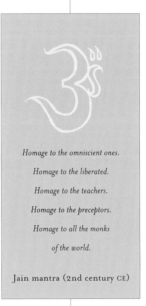

Homage to the omniscient ones.

Homage to the liberated.

Homage to the teachers.

Homage to the preceptors.

Homage to all the monks

of the world.

Jain mantra (2nd century CE)

Vibrational forces are believed to be particularly strong in the sequences of sounds that form mantras – these can be a powerful aid to concentration, whether repeated silently or chanted to gain the full benefit of their sound vibrations. Mantras usually consist of sacred words or texts, but they may simply be strings of syllables with no strict meaning. The meditator may repeat the mantra on each exhalation (the Buddhist monks sometimes chant on the inhalation as well) or use it independently of the breath. It can be used throughout meditation or returned to each time the mind is found wandering. A devotee reciting the sacred syllables is said to "absorb" the power incorporated in the sound of the words: by reciting the "root" mantra *Om*, he or she partakes of the power of creation.

There are different forms of mantra, such as the *bija* ("seed") mantras, which are thought to contain the energy pervading both the human body and the universe. In the Hindu and Buddhist traditions, mantras are usually associated with particular gods or Buddhas: Shiva, for example, is linked with *hrim*, and Kali with *krim*.

Many mantras are to be used only after initiation into them by a teacher of the lineage concerned. This initiation ensures correct pronunciation, and is said to transmit the mantra's secret inner power to the meditator. On occasions, the teacher will give the pupil a mantra for personal use, selecting it to suit the pupil's nature, experience and his or her particular needs. However, one of the best-known of all mantras, *Om Mani Padme Hum*, is regarded – like the sound *Om* – as so powerful that any sincere seeker can use it with benefit. Freely translated as "Hail to the Jewel in the Lotus", the mantra is designed to reveal one's true nature (the jewel), which resides within the spiritual centre or *chakra* (the lotus).

You can experiment with other sounds that require no initiation; for example, the Buddhist *So-ha*, the Moslem *Allah*, the Hebrew *Shalom*, or the Jesus Prayer of the Russian Orthodox Church (*Lord Jesus Christ, Son of God, have mercy on me a sinner*).

Using a Mantra

Exercise 20

The mantra *Om* – pronounced in three syllables "a-u-m" – is excellent not only in meditation, but also as a way of energizing and centring the body early each morning.

1. Sit comfortably and close your eyes. To help concentration, focus on the breath as usual.

2. Pronounce the first long "a" sound (a-r-r), allowing it to vibrate deep in your belly.

3. Pronounce the second "u" sound (o-o-o), allowing it to vibrate in the heart area.

4. Pronounce the third "m" sound (m-m-m) so that it vibrates in the so-called "third eye". Thus, both the sounds and the vibrations are felt to ascend through the body.

5. Repeat on long out-breaths at least a dozen times.

6. When you feel confident with the sounds and their vibrations, repeat the mantra on the in-breaths. Eventually progress to repeat on both the in- and out-breaths.

Creativity and Problem-solving

One of the greatest mysteries of the mind is the origin of thoughts. The more we watch our own thought processes in meditation, the more we become aware of this mystery. One moment the mind is empty, next moment, as if from nowhere, a thought appears — then another and another. Who or what puts together these strange mental events? Modern psychologists have no final answer. We say that thoughts emerge from the "unconscious", but this is simply to invent a term for mystery. The unconscious is as far beyond our direct comprehension as the invisible dark matter that holds the universe together, which eludes direct scientific observation.

The mystery that surrounds the origin of our thoughts is particularly apparent when it comes to creativity. Many creative artists have written of their creative processes, yet none has been able to explain their operation. A prime example is Mozart, who claimed to "hear" much of his music, so that he had only the task of writing it down. Where the music came from was as much a puzzle to him as it is to us. It is said that Shakespeare never had to correct a line he wrote — each one came to him ready-made. Many great scientists such as Poincaré, Mendeleyev and Bohr have also claimed that many insights came to them as if fully-formed from the unconscious, sometimes even in dreams.

There can be little doubt, however, that the more open we are to the inner world, the more readily creative thoughts and ideas are able to emerge into our consciousness. Meditation can be like "listening in" to some deep well within us — an imaginative spring that is capable of generating creative insights and impulses far beyond conscious thought. It is not surprising that the ancients thought these creative insights came from the gods.

One thing we can say is that creativity can be viewed as a form of problem-solving characterized by fluency and originality, whether the problem is to do with scientific invention, or with the idea for a play or a novel, or with the poetry needed to express a profound emotion. It is thus possible to meditate on a certain problem and listen for the answer. Whatever the problem, even if it is only a fairly mundane one, the process is the same. Keep the problem in your mind as you establish your meditation, as if confident that the solution will be found for you. Then let go of the problem, in the same way that you let go of all thoughts.

If solutions to the problem arise during meditation, instruct them to re-surface at the end of the meditation, then let them go. If you hold on to them, not only will you disrupt the rest of the meditation, you will prevent any further insights arising. If the required insights fail to appear, do not regard the exercise as a failure. They may arrive when least expected during the rest of the day, or be there when you wake the following morning.

Divine Inspiration

Many of the world's greatest works of art, from music and painting to spectacular cathedrals, were inspired by religious themes. Some of the most beautiful icons associated with the Greek and Russian Orthodox Churches were actually produced while the artists were in a state of consciousness in which the Divine vision was said to work directly through them. Western romantic poetry, which originated in the 13th century with the creative genius of the French troubadours, was initially a representation not of human love but of the mystical yearning of the soul for the Divine. The poetry of the Sufi mystics was similar in intent, while the union of male and female depicted in the stonework of some Indian temples represented the twin divine energies whose embrace created the visible world.

The Way of Paradox

One of the classic teachings in Buddhism is: "When the opposites arise, the Buddha-mind is lost." This teaching reveals that when we engage in oppositional thinking, we fragment the world into a collection of isolated, individual entities, and forfeit any sense of wholeness. Central to all the great Eastern traditions is that instead of thinking in terms of *either* this *or* that, we should see things as *both* this *and* that. For example, a cup is *both* form (the base and the sides) *and* space (the interior). Without both form and space there would be no cup. At a deeper level, the form encloses and defines the space, and the space (both inside and outside the cup) encloses and defines the form. Far from being opposites, form and space are thus an integral part of each other.

The spiritual life is full of such apparent paradoxes, which become less paradoxical the more we look into them. The concept of "emptiness" can be used to help explain this. All things are said to be "empty" of permanent, independent existence, and thus unified with each other in a beautiful and subtle web of interdependency.

Zen and the Koan

Zen Buddhism (more specifically, Rinzai Zen Buddhism) makes particular use of paradox to shake each individual out of habitual oppositional thinking, and into a deeper awareness of the real nature of existence. The *koan* is the main method of teaching by which paradox is presented, consisting as it does of a question to which there is no apparent answer, or of a nonsensical statement.

One of the best-known koans asks "What is the sound of one hand clapping?" Clapping is an activity carried out only by two hands, so surely the sound of one hand clapping must be silence? But then silence is the absence of sound. Or is it? Sound and silence, movement and stillness, height and depth — are they opposites or different aspects of the same thing? What is the meaning of "same" and "different"?

The meditator holds the koan in the forefront of the mind, as if putting it to a wise and loving friend who does not speak. "Do not ask the question of yourself," my Zen master instructed me. "Ask the koan." So the meditator puts the koan *to the koan* (another paradox). The koan cannot be answered by logic, as logic is the very tool of oppositional thinking. And the answer, when it comes, arrives not as logic but as a new way of seeing, a profound insight that at the same time is so simple that it may even prompt helpless laughter.

A resolution of this kind is not something that can be reduced to a

Words do not set forth facts,
Speech does not convey the spirit,
Those who take up words are lost;
Blocked by phrases one is confused.

Zen Master Mumon,
commenting on a koan

standard formula. Each answer must be put to the teacher for verification, and the teacher may reject from one meditator a resolution already accepted from another. It is not simply the words or gestures in which the resolution is expressed, but the mind from which they come that counts. The Zen masters' comments are often as enigmatic as the koans.

If you have a Rinzai Zen teacher, he or she will give you a suitable koan. When it is resolved, others will be given in ascending order of difficulty. Another example of a koan is *The Oak Tree in the Garden*. Zen Master Joshu was asked "Why did Bodhidharma come from the West?" – to which he replied: "The oak tree

in the garden." Bodhidharma was a 6th-century Indian Buddhist monk who took three years to make the journey to China and spent nine years meditating in front of a wall.

So what was the point of this dialogue, especially as Buddhism had arrived in China long before Bodhidharma? At one level, the question seems purely factual. But at a much deeper level it really asks: "What is the point of Buddhism?" Joshu's reply draws attention to the oak tree and thus to the natural world, but what is behind the natural world? Our minds use language and logic, but is either really equipped to come to terms with reality – for example, the essence of a tree?

see exercise overleaf

Working with a Koan

Exercise 21

Ideally, a meditation teacher will choose a koan for you (for example, *The Oak Tree in the Garden*, see p.131). If you have no tutor, choose a koan that sparks intrigue in you – one that you feel a strong desire to penetrate.

1. Resolve within yourself to persevere with your koan. Try not to be tempted into changing it if you have difficulty making progess toward a resolution. A teacher only permits change when the present koan is resolved. Frustration is all part of the exercise.

2. If the koan becomes too difficult, play with it and make friends with it as you may have done with difficult emotions. Don't worry if it seems unfathomable – you have no deadline by which you must solve its paradox. Remember, grim determination is not the only path to wisdom.

3. You can ponder your koan at times other than during meditation. Think of it as a wise old friend that you always have with you. "Speak" to it as often as you can, for example while travelling to work or working out in the gym.

4. Resolution cannot be verified without a teacher, but we can still gain important insights. If, after a time, these seem incomplete, you can go back to the koan for more help.

Zen in the Art of Everything

In addition to working with a koan, meditation can consist of direct contemplation (see *Exercise 6, The Improvised Meditation*, p.45), silent illumination (see *Exercise 11, Body Awareness*, p.71), and *kinhin* (see *Exercise 16, Kinhin*, p.113). Watching the breath is often used in conjunction with any or all of the above, and the practitioner may also use the technique of wall gazing, that is, sitting to face a blank wall, eyes open, with the attention focused unwaveringly upon whatever is in front. Care should be taken not to identify imaginary pictures or interesting abstract shapes in the texture of the wall, as the function of the meditation is to keep the mind as free of images as it is of thoughts.

However, as Zen is essentially a state of mind (or spirit), it permeates all aspects of life. Following the huge success of Eugene Herrigel's

---

Zen in the Art of Flower Arranging

The Zen art of flower arrangement has its origins in an early form of Zen garden – the aim was to capture the essence of a natural object, in this case nature itself. Only when the mind of the gardener was at one with nature was it possible for the garden to be as if it had grown by itself. Similarly, in flower arranging, nature is effortlessly present. The basis of Zen flower arrangement is the relationship between heaven, man and earth, which are all considered as states of mind. An arrangement has three main branches (a tall, central stem for heaven, a medium length stem for man, and a bent, short stem for earth). When these are properly placed they become a single branch, unfolding like a triangle. Each additional branch or flower supports or supplements heaven, man or earth.

illuminating book *Zen in the Art of Archery* (see p.112) a number of books with titles beginning *Zen in the Art of ...* by other authors have appeared, all attempting to show how the Zen mind can infuse and transform the most mundane tasks.

Essentially, the Zen mind is a

mind that can be totally absorbed in whatever it happens to be doing, with no ego (manifested in random thoughts and the consciousness of self as the doer of actions) intruding between spirit and activity. In this way spirit, activity and the object of activity become one. This state can sometimes be achieved when we are fully immersed in a pastime that involves harmony between mind and body and demands our whole attention. So if we are playing a sport, such as golf or tennis, we must focus the mind wholly on the present moment – the swing of the club or the position and direction of the ball as it approaches the racket.

It is said that the feeling of unity between mind, rhythmical physical activity, and outer world experienced by marathon runners is another glimpse into this Zen state, and the same may be true for the almost mystical experiences reported by individuals engaged in other endurance sports, such as long-distance swimming and cycling.

In many ways the concept of the Zen mind plays a part in all the great traditions, particularly where an emphasis is placed upon this inter-connectedness – or primal unity – of self, activity and other. We already know that this is true of Zen in the martial arts (see pp.111–13), but Zen also plays a part in such diverse pursuits as painting, calligraphy, the tea ceremony, poetry, garden design and flower arranging (see box, p.133). In painting, as an artist meditates on the subject of the work, he or she attains a state of oneness with it. The idea is that, once "oneness" is reached, the artist can capture the object's essence in a few deft brush strokes. No alterations are acceptable – the essence is there first time, or it is not there at all.

The Japanese tea ceremony, which is so often misunderstood in the West, is not merely a colourful and rather quaint old ritual, but a sequence of highly mannered movements, each of which flows into and gives rise to the next, thus demonstrating the interconnecedness of all things and allowing the prepared mind an intuitive grasp of the directness, simplicity and harmony of reality itself.

Zen poetry, which is best known through the 17-syllable Japanese *haiku*, is also devoted to conveying the inner essence of things. This essence, or "suchness" as it is sometimes called, simply "is". You either see it, or you do not. It reveals itself, constantly and continually, to the awakened mind.

Just as the Zen painter and the Zen poet accomplish their works of art in a single flow of heightened consciousness, so those who wish to grasp the suchness implicit in these artistic creations must also do so in the immediate moment. Zen art does not yield its "meaning" to analysis or to discussion. You either penetrate intuitively to the reality it portrays, or else the gateless gate remains closed to you.

The same is true when meditation takes place in the Zen garden, which consists only of rocks, stones and sand. Sometimes the sand is raked to represent ripples of water that are deflected here and there by the rocks and stones. These deflections show the distortion experienced when the ego becomes lost in *concepts* of reality instead of the experience in and of reality itself. When the meditator's awareness is focused upon the garden, the garden's essence is conveyed wordlessly to deep levels of the meditator's consciousness, enabling mind and garden to be recognized as one and the same experience, with all boundaries between seer and seen revealed as illusory.

Zen and the Meaning of Self

Zen has a habit of bringing us full circle. Like all the great traditions, it is not intended to transform the world, but to transform the mind that sees the world. This transformation can be likened to a perpetual journey around a circle — we come back to the same point time and time again, but with an enhanced insight and understanding. The American poet T.S. Eliot expresses a similar concept in "Little Gidding" (1942) when he says that the conclusion of our exploring is to "arrive where we started and know the place for the first time". A Zen saying further illustrates this idea: "I thought I had far to go, until I looked back and saw I had passed my destination many years before."

Before I studied Zen, mountains were mountains and rivers were rivers. Then I had my first Zen realizations, and mountains were no longer mountains and rivers were no longer rivers. Now that I have seen into Zen, mountains are once more mountains and rivers are once more rivers.

A Zen saying

These various words of wisdom all make the point that meditation (whether Zen or any other) does not transform us into new beings, but reveals to us what, in reality, we already are. It peels away the conditioned and artificial self that has been built up by the behaviour of others toward us, and by our own reactions to people and situations, and reconnects us with our essence — just as Zen art connects us with the essence of the objects it portrays. Ultimately, therefore, you are the answer to your own question, and journey and goal are inseparable. As a result, a meditation teacher, no matter how experienced, cannot possibly answer for you the ques-

tion "Who am I?" In addressing this question there is no substitute for personal experience. Even if we did not ask the question, the practice of meditation would soon ask it for us.

Beginners may fear that if the resolution of a Zen koan enables them to see through the superficial ego we mistake for ourselves, they may find there is nothing beyond. This fear can be exacerbated by the Buddhist teaching of *anatta*, or "no-self". *Anatta* is sometimes taken to mean that during life we have no permanent identity; and in the afterlife we are absorbed into an impersonal unity. The Hindu saying, "the dewdrop slips into the shining sea" gives a similar impression.

This over-simplification reveals the danger of trying to put the inexpressible into words. Our ultimate destiny lies *beyond* the opposites of individuality and unity. Every statement we make about such things is automatically wrong, as it attempts to limit what is limitless. Hence the emphasis should always be upon realization through personal experience. And if the mystics are to be believed, this realization is so splendid that all else pales into insignificance.

The
Outer Limits

Meditation takes us into the unknown territory of our own minds, and we might expect to meet some rather unusual experiences there. These often fall under the heading of psychic or paranormal. Many lie beyond the explanatory powers of modern science, but this is no reason to regard them simply as the result of self-delusion. The Buddha taught that we should take nothing others tell us about ourselves on trust, no matter how eminent they are as teachers. Only when we have put their teachings to the test can we know whether or not they are true for us.

We learn to be more attentive to life through meditation, and to notice signals and messages arising from our own minds that we would normally miss. The climate of thought surrounding us changes, and this in itself seems to facilitate so-called psychic experiences. However, the great traditions warn us not to use meditation as a way of seeking psychic powers. Such powers, if they arise, are a by-product of meditation rather than its goal, and are generally thought of as a grave distraction in that they risk feeding the ego rather than helping us to move beyond it.

Healing

Modern medicine at last accepts that the mind plays a role in physical illness. Some estimates suggest that as many as half the problems that hospitalize people may originate, at least partially, in psychological factors. If the mind is implicated in disease and disability, it follows that it can also play a part in healing. One way is through positive thinking and positive affirmation (see *Exercise 13, Positive Affirmation,* p.82), and another is by imagining oneself fit and strong and coping successfully with life. There is also a certain amount of evidence, even from Western medicine, that more spiritual methods can be very effective. Studies have shown that meditation can be helpful in relieving stress-related illnesses, and that patients who meditate following surgery are less likely to need pain-killers.

In the East, these inner methods have almost all been associated with the use of the breath. This involves not just the complete breath, but also the visualization of white light (see *Exercise 23, On the Shores of Sleep,* p.147). A simple method involves the meditator imagining white light flooding into the body on each in-breath and being directed to the area requiring healing on each out-breath. It is as if the lungs act as a pump, drawing healing energy in, then sending it flowing out to the trouble spot.

A more advanced technique is to visualize air drawn into the body not through the nostrils, but through other parts of the anatomy. Known typically as "heel breathing", the heels are in fact one of the best places to start the exercise. Either in the normal seated posture or lying flat on the back, the meditator visualizes white light being drawn in through his or her heels on the in-breath. The light is then visualized flowing spontaneously up the legs and then taking its course through the body directly toward the malady's centre. On the out-breath the light is seen leaving by the same route, taking the affliction with it. So, for

example, if we have a sprained left wrist, we might visualize the light travelling from the heels to the legs, up our torso and then down our left arm to the wrist.

Early on in this practice the meditator is likely to feel a sense of coolness at the heels and throughout the legs and abdomen as the white light is visualized being drawn into the body. It is unnecessary to speculate on whether this feeling is "real" or not. The point is that it is there. Equally, it is pointless to speculate whether any subsequent healing occurs as a direct result of heel breathing, or whether the heel breathing is simply a way of putting oneself into the requisite state of mind. The only result of such speculation is that the exercise is likely to be less beneficial in the future.

Once the meditator becomes proficient at the visualizations associated with heel breathing, the white light can be imagined drawn in through other parts of the body – the palms of the hands, the crown of the head, even the heart. In the more advanced exercises, and when specific disabilities are not being treated, the light can be seen setting each of the *chakras* (the yogic subtle-energy centres) spinning, and thus radiating multi-coloured energy throughout the body. To begin with, the heart chakra is often the easiest one to visualize in this way.

Altered States

Altered states of consciousness are experienced as a matter of routine during normal life. They are regularly induced by such things as sleep, tiredness, the trance-like state to which television can reduce us, moments of danger or high excitement, alcohol, caffeine and other drugs, and sustained physical exertion (particularly long-distance running). But meditation is perhaps the best example of all. The moment the mind switches into a calmer, more watchful state, the experience of one's own consciousness alters in a number of highly illuminating ways.

One of the main changes is in the field of memory. Often memories that have not consciously been entertained for years come into awareness, sometimes with such vividness that it is as though the recalled experiences are being re-lived. This recall can include memories of dreams that the meditator has previously been unable to recall – yet the conviction that they are dream memories is unshakeable.

Changes in body awareness also take place. Our consciousness of our own bodies is more tenuous than we think. In meditation there is sometimes a complete loss of this consciousness, as if the body has disappeared and the meditator is simply suspended in space. At other times the body may appear weightless; or as if the boundaries between the body and the rest of the world have disappeared; or as if the body expands or contracts to a minute point. These experiences should simply be noted, like any others in meditation, but their value is that they show the many ways in which consciousness can interact with physical reality.

The way in which we experience our emotional self can also change markedly in meditation. Even someone who is normally emotionally restrained may experience an almost overwhelming sense of compassion for all living creatures, or feelings of unselfish joy.

Sometimes the body may suddenly become sexually aroused, or may become full of a sense of vibrant energy. Again, the value of these experiences is that they indicate the potential we carry inside us for a whole range of rich, profound but often totally unexpected emotions.

Finally, if there is something more to human beings than a physical body, then there must be ways in which this "something more" can be directly experienced. A deepening awareness of one's spiritual nature sometimes arises spontaneously as meditation progresses. Known in the West as "oceanic" or mystical experiences, and in the East as *samadhi*, such experiences seem to have features in common in all the great traditions. They are extraordinarily blissful, and bring an unshakeable conviction that life does not actually end with death. Sometimes there is the awareness of yourself standing in the Divine presence (*savii kalpa samadhi*); sometimes all sense of self disappears and there is only the Divine (*nirvii kalpa samadhi*). But in both cases there is complete assurance that ultimate reality is unconditional love.

Right and Left Hemispheres

The right hemisphere of the brain tends to control the left side of the body and plays a greater part in creative, imaginative and mystical experiences. The left hemisphere controls the right side and has a primary role in language and logical thinking. Most people emphasize the right side of their bodies (for example, they are right-handed), and thus usually the left hemisphere of their brains.

By bringing the body into greater balance through meditation, we can help to utilize the right hemisphere. If we are left-handed, we tend to emphasize the right hemisphere of the brain – and by achieving a greater sense of inner balance help to utilize the left hemisphere. Through greater inner balance and utilization of both sides of the brain we may begin to tap into the inner space that lies dormant.

---

see exercise overleaf

Balancing the Self

Exercise 22

Spiritual and mystical experiences arise in meditation as if by grace. This exercise aims to help general receptivity to altered states by achieving a greater sense of inner balance.

1. Sit comfortably and close your eyes. To help concentration, watch the breath until body and mind become still and relaxed.

2. If you are right-handed, concentrate on the left side of your body, particularly your left hand and left foot. Visualize yourself walking toward a door. Imagine that you reach out with your left hand and turn the handle. (If you are left-handed, concentrate on the right side.)

3. Now, in your mind's eye, begin to walk through the doorway, being mindful of taking the first step with your left foot. As you pass through the doorway, turn toward the left and close the door using your left hand again.

4. Once you have finished this visualization, spend a few moments imagining powerful energy coursing up your left side. Try to bring this increased emphasis on your left side into your life.

Meditation and Dreaming

This book places emphasis on the fact that meditation is not a sleepy or trance-like state. It may therefore seem strange to link meditation with dreaming. Yet all the Eastern traditions (and Western mystery traditions) teach that in the advanced meditator, conscious awareness runs continuously, not only throughout his or her waking life, but through dreams and even through dreamless sleep. In short, there are never any moments of oblivion. The Tibetan Buddhist idea that sleep is a dress rehearsal for death is linked to this teaching. If we can remain aware throughout sleep, we therefore remain aware as we pass through death, with the result that we have far greater control over what happens to us in the next world.

Awareness in dreams – that is, the recognition that we are dreaming and can consciously influence our dream experiences – is known in the West as *lucid dreaming*. The lucid dreamer experiences a wonderful expansion of dream consciousness, and can use the dream to fly, to visit desired locations, to find a spiritual teacher, or whatever he or she may wish. The dream still sets each of these scenes, but it is the dreamer who makes the initial decisions.

Consciousness in dreamless sleep is akin to profound meditation, in which the mind is free of thoughts and images, and experiences instead the profound clarity of contentless awareness.

These sleep states will begin to occur naturally as you make progress in your meditation practice. Lucid dreams, in particular, may come quite early on (although perhaps only occasionally). The meditator's increased mindfulness in waking life is carried over into sleep, so that he or she notices the anomalies that occur in dreams, and realizes in consequence that a dream is taking place. However, the development of lucid dreaming can be hastened if you ask yourself the question during the day, "How do I know this is not a dream?" Look around you carefully before you answer. Is it the familiarity and predictability of your waking life? Is it the fact that you can read, and that when you re-read the same passage, the words remain the same? Is it that you can make clear decisions and think logically? Is it that you can tell the time of day? Remind yourself that when you fail to be able to do these things, you will recognize that you are in fact dreaming.

Other strategies for hastening lucid dreaming are to tell yourself that the next time you do something that occurs frequently in your dreams it will remind you that you are dreaming. Or perhaps there are certain objects or places that often appear in your dreams – they, too, can be your cues into lucid dreaming. (It may be helpful to note them down immediately upon waking – you could then try to imagine some of the objects and focus upon them before you go to bed, telling yourself that these will be your lucidity triggers.) Alternatively, simply tell yourself before going to sleep or when the mind is in a meditative state, that you will know when you dream. Commercial devices that alert you when you are entering dreamful sleep can also be a help. Strapped to your wrist, these emit a small electric pulse that should not wake you but simply startle you into an awareness of dreaming.

Many of us have at some time experienced a "false awakening", and this can be a perfect opportunity to trigger our dreams into lucidity. False awakenings tend to occur when we are on the verge of truly waking up: we become aware that we must soon get out of bed and so begin to dream, with vivid reality, of our morning routine, while at the same time being strangely aware of still being in bed.

The experience of lucid dreaming adds an extraordinary dimension to normal consciousness. The ancients thought that it indicated the ability to travel on the astral planes and to visit other worlds. Although this may seem to us naïve, there is no doubt that lucid dreaming extends our self-knowledge, and our understanding of the unsuspected abilities of the mind.

On the Shores of Sleep

Exercise 23

A Tibetan Buddhist practice that helps consciousness to run continuously from waking life into sleep is to meditate upon a spinning disk of white light near our hearts. This can be done either during your meditation sessions or when you are in bed, drifting off to sleep.

1. Focus upon your breath and then transfer your awareness to your heart. You may be aware of it beating, or you may simply focus upon the space where it sits.

2. Now visualize – and try to sense at the same time – the presence of a disk of still white light, with its centre at the heart and its circumference extending a little beyond it.

3. Now set the disk spinning, slowly at first, then gradually gathering speed. As it spins faster, you may have the impression of rainbow colours merging together to form the white light. You may find the exercise tends to delay sleep for the first few nights. In which case, try not to concentrate too hard. Try to be conscious of the presence of the disk, rather than of any sense that you are responsible for its presence. If possible, fall asleep with the disk still spinning.

In and Out of the Body

Lucid dreaming is regarded by some writers as a halfway house toward what are known as "Out of Body Experiences" (OBEs). These are occasions in which consciousness seems to leave the body, and exist independently of it. Sometimes the individual can see his or her physical body lying on the bed or sitting in the chair, while the conscious body has the ability to disobey normal laws and pass through walls. At other times, some people feel as if they are in a clever copy of the real world, or sometimes even in other dimensions, as tends to happen if the OBE occurs during a near-death experience. In the latter instance, people report seeing deceased relatives waiting to greet them, and are sent back to their bodies because their time to die has not yet come.

The great meditative traditions teach that OBEs happen when the soul temporarily parts from the physical body, and they maintain that such experiences are evidence of the non-material nature of the real self. Some Western scientists dismiss OBEs as hallucinations, or as effects of the dying brain, but there is no doubt that they feel real enough to the participants who actually undergo them. In many cases OBEs also lead to long-standing changes in the way in which the individual thinks about him or herself, and about the survival of physical death.

On occasions, meditators report OBEs during periods of intensive practice, and it may be that meditation greatly increases the chances of such things happening. Suddenly, the meditator may be looking down at him or herself upon the meditation cushion, and may note features of personal appearance that have not previously been observed. The experience can bring feelings of panic, and fears that one may have died and not be able to return to the body. However, the simple wish to be back is usually sufficient to produce the desired effect.

There is no doubt that a single OBE can be a life-transforming experience. However, the great traditions teach that it should not become an aim in meditation. It cannot be stressed too strongly that meditation is a process of observation of what happens, whether it be normal or extraordinary, rather than a way of making things happen.

In the East, paranormal powers are described as the *siddhis*, and it is taken for granted by many traditions that they are a natural by-product of meditation, probably as a result of the meditator's greater awareness of the subtle messages arising within the mind. Normally, the mind's mental chatter, together with its orientation primarily toward the outside world, prevents these signals from arising into consciousness.

The *siddhis* take various forms, but the ones most widely recognized in the West are the ability to read the thoughts of others (telepathy), the ability to gain information about the external world other than through the senses (clairvoyance), the ability to gain knowledge of the future (precognition) and the ability to move external objects by the power of thought (psychokinesis). We may wish to discount some stories about these abilities, but there is evidence from controlled laboratory experiments that to a limited extent such abilities do exist.

Not all meditators develop the *siddhis*, and the great traditions teach that you should never seek them. They are not to be regarded as an indication of spiritual development and they should never deflect the meditator from the serious business of meditation itself. But they do indicate significant progress in at least the mind training that comes as a result of meditation, and in this sense they are useful.

The *siddhis* may show themselves in many different ways. For example, you may find yourself suddenly aware, when you visit a place for the first time, that you have been there before; or you may have a novel experience, and yet feel that you have lived through it before — an experience known as *déjà vu*.

Conclusion

No single book can hope to say all there is to say about meditation. The practice is the most profound method of exploring the mind and plumbing the mysteries of being known to humankind. The serious meditator never stops learning – from teachers, from fellow meditators, from books, and from his or her own experience of life. Like a journey during which every turn of the road opens up new vistas, meditation reveals insight after insight as it takes us ever deeper into ourselves. The practice of meditation is without doubt a path without end.

I would like to conclude this book by emphasizing once more that *anyone* can meditate. Meditation is not something that is exclusive to ascetics, or to those who are able to devote days or weeks at a time to going on retreats. Neither should you be misled into thinking that because your mind seems restless and untamed, meditation is not for you. It is precisely because of this restlessness that we need to meditate. And do not be discouraged if, after apparently making good progress, you suddenly find that you seem to have slipped back to the beginning again. This is something that, at one time or another, happens to us all, and it is during these seemingly disheartening experiences that meditation becomes even more important. Patience, and a calm but steadfast determination to sit with the confusion, are the things that count most at such times.

On other occasions, you may feel that you have reached a plateau from which you seem to make no further progress – even despite the fact that your awareness of your breath or of a mantra has not left you. When this happens, just as when your thoughts persist in dominating the centre of your awareness, try to be patient. Since early childhood and our first lessons at school, most of us have become used to the idea that to learn any skill involves steady, recognizable progress that

is marked by the ability to tick off each milestone as we reach it. Our experience of this form of learning leads us to expect that the same thing will happen when we take up meditation. But in meditation such orderly progress proves all too often to be impossible. This is simply the nature of the mind, and the more we go into our minds the more we recognize how subtle and elusive they are, and the more we appreciate the extent to which they refuse to conform to the logicalities and predictabilities of the external world.

Do not expect miracles, but keep one thought always before you – you *can* meditate. Remember, too, that you will learn more about yourself from meditation than you will from observations that others have made about you, or from keeping a diary, or from looking in a mirror. By reading this book you have begun your journey – or continued it if you are already on the path – through the gateless gate that opens onto a new, yet perhaps strangely familiar, domain of tranquillity, clarity and discovery.

"Who am I?" is the most important question that we can ask ourselves. It is the simplest and at the same time the most subtle and complex question. To answer it, follow the advice of the old meditation masters, which is as relevant today as it ever was: "Start – and continue."

Bibliography

The following is a brief guide to books
on meditation and related topics.

Meditation

Fontana, D. *The Elements of Meditation*,
Element Books, Shaftesbury
(England) and Boston, 1991

Fontana, D. *The Meditator's Handbook*,
Element Books, Shaftesbury
(England) and Boston, 1992

McDonald, K. *How to Meditate*, Wisdom
Books, New York, 1984

Steinbrecher, E.C. *The Inner Guide to
Meditation*, Samuel Weiser, London
and New York, 1994

Symbols

Fontana, D. *The Secret Language of Symbols*,
Chronicle Books, San Francisco,
1993; Piatkus, London, 1997

The Koan

Cleary, J.C. *Meditating with Koans*, Asian
Humanities Press, Berkeley, 1992

Visualization

Gawain, S. *Creative Visualization*, Bantam
Books, New York, 1982

Dreams

Fontana, D. *The Secret Language of Dreams*,
Chronicle Books, San Francisco,
1994; Piatkus, London, 1997

Fontana, D. *Teach Yourself to Dream*,
Chronicle Books, San Francisco,
1997; DBP/Mitchell Beazley, 1997

Yoga

Hewitt, J. *The Complete Yoga Book*, Rider,
London, 1987; new edition Leopard
Books, 1995

The Great Traditions

Coogan, M.D. (ed.) *World Religions*,
Oxford University Press, New York,
1998; Duncan Baird Publishers,
London, 1998

Out of Body Experiences

Peterson, R. *Out of Body Experiences*,
Hampton Roads, Charlottesville,
1997

Psychic Abilities

Duncan, L. and Roll, W. *Psychic
Connections*, Delacorte Press, New York,
1995

Index

C r e d i t s

The publishers would like to thank the following for permission to reproduce their material.

Page 81
British Library, London.
Pages 93 and **94**
Christie's Images.
Page 97
Victoria & Albert Museum, London.
Page 101
Images Colour Library.
Page 110
Duncan Baird Publishers.
Page 116
Images Colour Library.